The sales manager's desktop guide

Mike Gale and Julian Clay

Published by Hawksmere
12-18 Grosvenor Gardens
London SW1W 0DH.
www.hawksmere.co.uk

© Mike Gale and Julian Clay 2000

All rights reserved. No part of this publication may be reproduced, stored in a retrieval system or transmitted in any form or by any means, electronic, photocopying, recording or otherwise, without the prior permission of the publisher.

This book is sold subject to the condition that it shall not, by way of trade or otherwise, be lent, re-sold, hired out or otherwise circulated without the publisher's prior consent in any form of binding or cover other than in which it is published and without a similar condition including this condition being imposed upon the subsequent purchaser.

No responsibility for loss occasioned to any person acting or refraining from action as a result of any material in this publication can be accepted by the authors or publisher.

Crown copyright is reproduced with the permission of the Controller of Her Majesty's Stationery Office.

A CIP catalogue record for this book is available from the British Library.

ISBN 1 85418 129 7

Printed in Great Britain by Ashford Colour Press.

Designed and typeset by Driftdesign for Hawksmere.

About the authors

Mike Gale

Mike Gale graduated from Leeds University with an honours degree in Management Studies and Languages. He began his career with Standard Chartered Bank and was a Senior Regional Team Leader with the Thomas Cook Group, marketing and selling to banknote operations in the UK, Europe and the Middle East.

He has been a training consultant and motivational speaker for conference events in the UK and around the world for ten years.

Mike has worked with over 100 companies in the public and private sector including, Vodafone, Braun [UK], McKinsey & Co, the DTI, and the BBC.

Thanks

I would like to express my gratitude to Noreen Clifford of Hawksmere, who recommended me for this project and introduced me to a new and challenging opportunity.

Also, a special thank you to my wife Trudy, and my daughter Christy, for their patience and understanding.

Julian Clay

Since leaving the University of North London with a Higher National Diploma in Business Studies, Julian Clay has had a successful sales career for over fifteen years.

Most of this time was spent in territory sales and key account management with the office imaging division of Kodak. Here he gained a valuable insight into how sales people are managed. His ability to continually exceed annual targets was rewarded in 1995 when he became the top sales performer in the UK.

Julian has developed models in the areas of account management, forecasting and sales performance. He is now a consultant who helps companies increase their revenue by managing their sales operation more effectively.

He has worked with companies in direct sales and indirect channels. Some of these include Danka UK plc, ICI Imagedata, Racal Airtech and the James McNaughton Paper Group.

Thanks

I would like to thank Martin Clay, for his invaluable help in structuring the chapters and for his feedback as a sales manager; to Doug Dews for giving me the benefit of his vast experience as a former sales manager and to Andrew Mills for his detailed contribution on selling through indirect channels.

A special thank you to Tina Thorne for her support and for taking the time to help with editing.

Julian Clay and Mike Gale can provide a comprehensive range of sales consultancy, training and coaching services.

CONTENTS

Introduction 1
Managing yourself 2

Leadership 9
Introduction 10
Understanding leadership 10
Leadership styles 16
Leading the team 20
Delegation 22
Chapter summary 26
Checklist 26

Sales planning 27
Introduction 28
A sales manager's plan 28
Territory planning 31
Sales targets 35
Forecasting future sales 38
Chapter summary 43
Checklist 44

Managing your accounts 45
Introduction 46
Understanding account management 46
Call plan management 53
Applying account management skills 57
Chapter summary 60
Checklist 60

Contents

4 Building business relationships 61
Introduction 62
Managing at all levels 62
Focusing on the customer 68
Chapter summary 70
Checklist 70

5 Managing the sale 71
Introduction 72
Stages of the sales cycle 72
Analysing sales behaviour 75
Monitoring activity and performance 82
Chapter summary 86
Checklist 86

6 Communication and development 87
Introduction 88
Behavioural styles 88
Appraisal 94
Coaching 103
Chapter summary 107
Checklist 107

7 Motivating the team 109
Introduction 110
An individual's goals 110
Motivation theory and practice 112
Influencing behaviour and attitudes 118
Motivation and reward 125
Chapter summary 129
Checklist 129

Contents

8 Personal effectiveness 131
Introduction 132
Planning and prioritising 132
Effective daily routines 137
Improving your time management skills..............................143
Improving your overall effectiveness 144
Chapter summary..147
Checklist 148

9 Managing change 149
Introduction 150
Factors affecting change..150
Analysing a need for change...154
Resistance to change 157
Involving people in the change process 161
Chapter summary 164
Checklist 164

10 Recruitment 165
Introduction 166
Defining the sales role 166
Setting parameters 169
Assessment 170
Interviewing and induction...176
Chapter summary 180
Checklist 180

11 Selling through indirect channels 181
Introduction 182
Challenges and benefits 182
Managing indirect channels 185
Chapter summary 189
Checklist 189

Icons

Throughout the Desktop Guide series of books you will see references and symbols in the margins. These are designed for ease of use and quick reference directing you to key features of the text. The symbols used are:

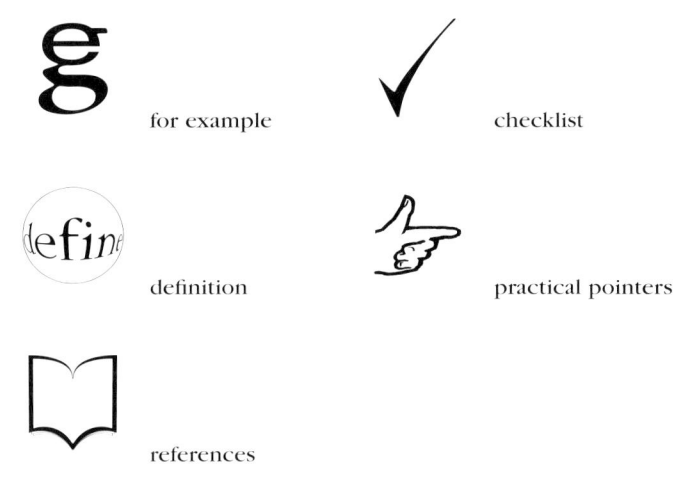

g   for example

✓   checklist

define   definition

☞   practical pointers

📖   references

Introduction

Managing yourself

Introduction

This book is intended to be a practical guide on how to deal with the many challenges you will face as a sales manager. We hope that you are able to apply many of the sales models to your own market and role.

The word 'planning' will appear many times in this book. This is because it is an important part of preparing for success. Preparation means looking at ways in which you as a (prospective) sales manager can manage the task ahead. In order to achieve this you will need to consider how you manage yourself.

Managing yourself

Effective managers consistently help their sales team achieve results. They do this by managing their time (and their salespeople) well. They also focus on the correct aspects of their role. This will depend on a number of factors:

- Your personal style
- The directives from your immediate manager
- Your company's goals
- The products you sell
- The market you are in.

A successful sales manager has respect for other people's time. Whatever pressures you may be under you must be able to remain objective and be part of a team.

There will be many aspects to your role and it is the ability to combine them that will determine your level of success.

The role

There are three main areas that will be fundamental to your success. These are the ability to be a good:

1. Leader
2. Communicator
3. Business person.

These qualities are related to each other and will call for different uses depending on the situation. For a sales manager, the challenge will be to understand how and when to use them in the sales environment.

Limitations to the role

While you will need to be adaptable there will be many factors that may be outside your control. These can affect the performance of the sales team and your own level of motivation. Some examples include:

- Legal factors
- Line management
- Staff behaviour
- Technological factors
- Geographical factors
- Company policy
- Resources available to you
- Customer attitude/behaviour
- Market/demand
- Product/service.

It is important to recognise that you will have to accept some of these limitations and remain focused on what you can do. They are there to test you, not to defeat you.

Introduction

You will have to manage them on a daily basis, though it is unlikely they will all occur at the same time. If you can try to anticipate their effect and make the best of the situation, you have a greater chance of managing them well.

What type of manager are you?

When you begin a role as a sales manager it is important to look at:

- The type of person you are
- The type of manager you would like to be.

You need to consider your own strengths and weaknesses. You will also need to decide how involved you plan to be with your sales team, as you will probably have had a great deal of sales experience. Some of the questions you may want to ask yourself before you begin in the role include:

- Can you remain outside the direct sales team and manage it without interference?
- Can you be objective about how someone else is performing if they do things differently to you?

Being honest with yourself will help you manage others more effectively.

You will also need to look at:

- The task you have been given
- The degree of control you have over it
- The extent of your responsibility.

Your perception of the sales manager's role may differ from other peoples. You will need to define and take control of your areas of responsibility. As with most selling situations, you can achieve this by having patience, enthusiasm and determination and also showing initiative.

Introduction

Your manager

Your level of success will depend on the way you work with:

- The sales team
- Your manager.

Having a good relationship with your own manager will be an important factor in determining your level of motivation and success. In the same way that you may offer help to a sales person, you may also need help from your manager.

This can be done by ensuring that you:

- Have a clear understanding of how you are expected to interpret your company's business objectives
- Have regular meetings with him/her (to get confirmation that objectives are being met)
- Receive feedback on how well you are managing your sales team
- Communicate any concerns about achieving your sales target (and about anything you feel may stop you managing your sales people effectively)
- Understand your line manager's goals and area of responsibility.

Having a good relationship with other senior managers in your company will also help. This will encourage colleagues in different departments to work with you for the same company objectives.

Being a good manager is about your ability to:

- Persuade
- Succeed
- Listen
- Lead
- Work under pressure
- Motivate
- Communicate
- Work well with people

Introduction

- Be open minded
- Focus (on the task ahead)
- Learn new skills
- Adapt to change.

You have more chance of developing your management skills if you know how to get the best out of yourself. Being well prepared, having a good understanding of your market and the team of people you lead will help you.

Selling is both challenging and rewarding. Above all, your interpretation of the various topics discussed in this book may determine how you apply them. We hope that you remain positive and manage your sales team in a way that you would like to be managed.

The following table will enable the reader to find a personal route through the book. You may wish to refer to the chapter headings for an indication of the subjects covered. In the first column we have selected topics that may be of particular interest to you. By marking your priority in the second column you can devise your preferred order of reading material.

Introduction

Subject reference table

SUBJECT	PRIORITY	CHAPTER	PAGES
Different leadership styles		Chapter one – Leadership Leadership styles	16-20
Delegation		Chapter one – Leadership Delegation	22-25
		Chapter eight – Personal effectiveness Effective daily routines	137-142
Setting achievable targets		Chapter two – Sales planning Sales targets	35-37
Accurate forecasting		Chapter two – Sales planning Forecasting future sales	38-43
Winning and maintaining accounts		Chapter three – Managing your accounts Applying account management skills	57-60
Raising your levels of contact		Chapter four – Building business relationships Managing at all levels	62-67
Monitoring sales performance		Chapter five – Managing the sale Monitoring activity and performance	82-85
Communicating with different types of people		Chapter six – Communication and development Behavioural styles	88-94
Positive communication techniques		Chapter seven – Motivating the team Influencing behaviour and attitudes	118-124
Improving time management		Chapter eight – Personal effectiveness Planning and prioritising	132-136
Getting people to accept new ideas		Chapter nine – Managing change Involving people in the change process	161-164
How to select the right people		Chapter ten – Recruitment Assessment	170-176

chapter 1

Leadership

Introduction

Understanding leadership

Leadership styles

Leading the team

Delegation

Chapter summary

Checklist

Leadership

chapter 1

Introduction

The sales manager's role has two important elements to it:

1. To achieve sales targets (in line with the company's business objectives)
2. To manage and develop their sales people.

How can sales managers get a high performance from their team, in order to succeed in their role and achieve the above objectives? One key aspect will be the manner in which they lead.

In this chapter we will look at the practical steps sales managers can take to:

- Demonstrate leadership skills (to help sales people exceed their targets)
- Use different communication styles (to help people with different levels of ability and experience)
- Develop skills through delegation (to encourage sales people to contribute to the team and meet their personal goals).

Understanding leadership

In this section we will define leadership and distinguish it from management. If a sales manager is also a good leader they will bring three main benefits to the sales team:

1. A positive attitude that encourages loyalty and a desire to perform.
2. A good working atmosphere.
3. Better working relationships – by having clearly defined goals and levels of expectation.

Leadership

chapter 1

Defining leadership

Leadership means providing consistent, clear direction to your team.

As a sales manager you will be judged on results. This will test your ability to:

- Assess (and interpret the challenges facing your sales team)
- Communicate (these challenges and find ways to overcome them)
- Create the right atmosphere for the sales team to perform
- Support your sales people.

There are many ways for a sales manager to be an effective leader. Some characteristics that are commonly seen in leaders are:

Vision and anticipation	How you see the sales team developing and anticipating what might happen in the future
Integrity and honesty	Representing the principles that your team will respect
Self-belief	Encouraging other sales people to believe in themselves
Being objective	Being realistic and fair (completing tasks, admitting any mistakes you make and correcting them)
Innovation	Looking at ways of doing things better and trying new ideas
Listening and communicating	Involving the team, communicating with them regularly and incorporating their suggestions

Differences between sales leadership and management

It is the combination of leadership and management that creates a successful sales manager. What is the difference between leadership and management?

- **Management means organising the activities of the people who directly report to you**

The focus is more on the task – getting the job done.

- **Leadership is about creating an environment where people can get results**

The focus is more on the people – encouraging the right behaviour.

Management and leadership are both about getting results. Managing a sales team means that you need to lead it too.

There is pressure in sales management to meet and exceed company targets. A good sales manager will ensure that he/she:

- Focuses on *how* they lead their team
- Manages the tasks in order to meet the target.

How you manage your team will affect their success in meeting the overall sales targets. A measure of your leadership style will be your ability to balance the focus on the task with your focus on the people you manage.

Context, character and attitude

The starting point for effective leadership in sales management is to address:

1. **The context (of the situation you face)**
2. **Your character**
3. **Your attitude.**

Let us look at each of these three characteristics individually.

Context

Looking at the context of a situation will include a number of elements. It will depend on whether you:

- Follow the company's sales plan properly
- Regularly assess the effectiveness of the sales team (to fit in with the plan)
- Look at current market forces to assess realism of sales forecasts.

Sales people can work more effectively if they understand some of the areas that affect their sales performance. A sales manager needs to interpret the company's sales plans and communicate relevant information to the team. This can be used to address different aspects of performance, for example:

- Factors affecting sales targets (and what needs to be done)
- The impact of any developments on customers
- The way sales people are working internally with other parts of your company.

Character

Character is about self-knowledge and understanding what principles are important to you. It covers issues like:

- What you value most in being effective at work
- Honesty
- How good you are at keeping to your commitments
- Being structured and well organised.

Elements of your character will be noted and copied by your sales team. A leader sets the standard for others to follow. You should be aware of what fundamental issues you agree with so that you can communicate these to the members of your team. This will help create respect for your role and give people a high standard of behaviour to follow.

Attitude

Attitude is about how you think and behave. It is affected by how you feel. This, in turn, can affect how you manage your sales people and what you say to them.

Your attitude will determine:

- What you say
- How you say it
- How you respond to the needs of others
- What mood you are in.

Your attitude is what defines you today. It is about the type of person you are and about other people's perception of you.

The context of your existing situation, your character and your attitude towards the people that you manage are important elements to consider as a leader. By being aware of these three leadership areas you should find it easier to manage your sales people.

Self-development

One way to develop your own style of leadership is to think about the qualities you have and to list them. Although this is subjective it will give you the opportunity to focus on what your strengths are. This can be looked at in more detail in the following way:

Step 1

List as many qualities as you can that you would associate with a successful leader. Think of people you know and admire, historical or contemporary. Note what you admire about them and which qualities you see as effective.

Step 2

From this, you may then want to decide which three leadership elements of your own character to focus on. For example, you might decide to be more **patient**, **helpful** or **assertive**.

Step 3

By being aware of the leadership characteristics you want to adapt you can measure yourself more easily in different situations. This will give you focus and help you to be more aware of how you deal with people.

These qualities will form a key element to you using your influence and authority effectively. This will come essentially from a combination of three sources:

- **Status** (your position in the company)
- **Knowledge** (your level of experience)
- **Attitude** (being positive/personal attributes).

While status and knowledge are important, it is the third element that will make you a role model to your sales team.

If you are consistent and positive in your communication to others your colleagues will find it easier to work with you. This will give them a reason to respect you and your style of leadership.

An important leadership challenge many managers face is to understand the connection between:

- What you want – (results)
- How you want to manage – (behaviour).

Understanding your own leadership qualities and aspirations will make you more aware of when and how you use them successfully.

Leadership

Leadership styles

Effective leadership in the sales management role is often about good communication skills. We will now consider how a sales manager can lead in a way that will help sales people to produce the results they aim for.

You can develop your communication skills in three ways:

1. Assessing what level of control you use - leadership style.
2. Adapting to different people you communicate with (see Chapter 6 – Communication and development – behavioural styles).
3. Adjusting the manner in which you are communicating with someone (see Chapter 7 – Motivating the team – influencing behaviour and attitudes).

There are different ways to lead the sales team. In this section we will:

- Identify the range of leadership styles to use
- Establish which one to use (depending on the situation).

Your leadership style will be influenced by the type of person you are and the circumstances you face. Your effectiveness will be determined partly by how well you are able to adapt your style of leadership.

The four leadership styles

We will describe four leadership styles and look at which one you could adopt depending on the sales situation you face. There are two extremes to consider:

Supportive  Forcing

The **Supportive** style incorporates the following elements:

- Praise and encouragement
- Being helpful and providing suggestions
- Listening and understanding
- Allowing the individual to make their own decisions.

The **Forcing** style makes clearer demands. It requires:

- Control, structure and being decisive
- Direction and guidance
- Written communication
- Regular monitoring (to ensure that any agreed actions are completed).

There are times when a manager will not need (or feel comfortable using) the extremes of these styles. Most of the challenges they face require a style that is somewhere between the two.

You will also need to take your own personality into account when deciding upon a correct course of action. If you are a strong willed person you may want to balance this with a more supportive approach. Someone with a naturally supportive style might want to be more assertive where appropriate.

These more moderate communication styles can be divided into two categories:

Supportive – Forcing

Focuses on the same areas as supportive but requires elements of the forcing style.

Forcing – Supportive

Focuses on the same areas as forcing but requires elements of the supportive style.

The four leadership styles are illustrated below:

Supportive ◄——► **Supportive – Forcing** ◄——► **Forcing – Supportive** ◄——► **Forcing**

A sales manager might use one style as opposed to another depending on:

- The type of person he/she is
- The type of person he/she is communicating with
- The current situation
- Directives from senior management
- How well the sales targets are being met.

Interpreting the styles

It is difficult to indicate the right style to use for every sales situation. However, in the table below we describe the four leadership styles and provide some examples of how they can be interpreted. This will depend on the individual and the context of the situation.

Communication style	Objective	Examples of when to use
Supportive		
Less time spent with person, regular acknowledgement, and goals with long timeframes.	Your aim is to give the sales person a certain amount of freedom. This allows them to perform without instruction from you.	1. The sales person is experienced and performing well. He/she is demonstrating the right effort and selling skills. 2. The sales person may be under-performing but you have a good knowledge of their ability. You have given them a task that he/she should be able to achieve.
Supportive – Forcing		
Some time spent with the sales person, regular acknowledgement and follow-up with longer timeframes.	Your aim is to remain flexible with the sales person while introducing an element of guidance. Advice is given from you on how a situation might be solved.	1. The sales person may be performing well but you have identified an aspect of their behaviour (skill, effort, and attitude) that needs improving. 2. The sales person is under-performing and you wish to provide guidance and advice to help them.
Forcing – Supportive		
More time spent with the sales person. Regular acknowledgement and follow-up with shorter timeframes.	Your aim is to deal with an issue using a more direct approach. This may be combined with instruction, guidance and positive co-operation.	1. The sales person is performing well, but may not have implemented your previous suggestions properly. 2. The sales person is under-performing and you are taking corrective action. You are communicating what is needed and how it can be done.
Forcing		
More time spent with the sales person; written objectives; regular meetings and short timeframes.	Your aim is to confront, control, direct and demand action with no flexibility.	1. The sales person is performing well, but is setting a bad example to other members of the team. 2. The sales person is under-performing and has failed to implement your previous instructions.

Figure 1: Interpreting leadership styles

Flexibility of style

The challenge you face is to assess how to handle different combinations of performance. This can be managed well if you begin by setting standards of acceptable sales behaviour. This will show that you are consistent and flexible in most situations. The chart below is designed to provide you with further guidance on the choice of styles:

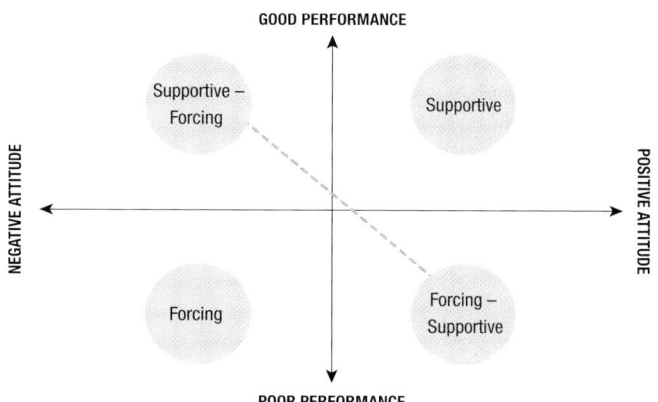

Figure 2: Choosing a leadership style

- If you have someone consistently meeting his/her sales target with a positive attitude, you might allow greater flexibility in your style.

- Conversely, poor performance and lack of commitment may require a more disciplined, direct approach. This might include specific, targeted areas for improvement and supervision.

As a sales manager you will need to monitor a sales person's attitude/motivation and performance to be able to set the correct standards.

The benefit of doing this is that it will encourage you to be consistent and to use the extreme leadership styles for the right reasons. Using the Forcing/Supportive styles can occur because of your mood and this might affect the attitude of your sales team.

Leadership

chapter 1

A sales manager's main goal is to be able to move from one style (up/down) to another depending on the situation. If you are supportive in your style at the beginning and it is not working, move up to the next style. This illustrates your desire to solve the problem and shows your strength of commitment.

We have looked at different forms of communication a sales manager can adopt to suit individual circumstances. Which style you use, and how you communicate with members of your sales team, will influence their level of motivation. This will depend on the attitude of your sales people and of yourself. It will also depend on how well they are performing.

Leading the team

Adopting the right team leadership style will differ depending on the context of the situation. A sales manager's intuition also plays a part in this. There are a number of elements that will affect the outcome. For example:

- The sales manager's level of interaction with the team
- His/her experience
- The strength of the personalities in the team.

With proper thought and planning you can demonstrate good leadership skills. Above all, it is your behaviour that will inspire your team.

Team assessment

The leadership styles (Supportive through to Forcing) we looked at earlier can be easily applied to a group of sales people as well as an individual. A sales manager will need to assess which leadership style is appropriate to the team.

This will depend on a number of factors, including:

1. The current state of motivation and attitude of the team.
2. The level of effort and application (being shown by each team member).

Leadership

chapter 1

3. The trend of recent sales results.
4. The gap between expected and actual results.
5. The stability and experience of the team.
6. External factors (changes in your market, mergers and new competitors).

A manager can assess each factor to build a balanced perception of the team. This will then influence the style they decide to adopt.

In the table below, we have divided each heading into four graded descriptions. In each column a manager has selected the description that most closely relates to their team.

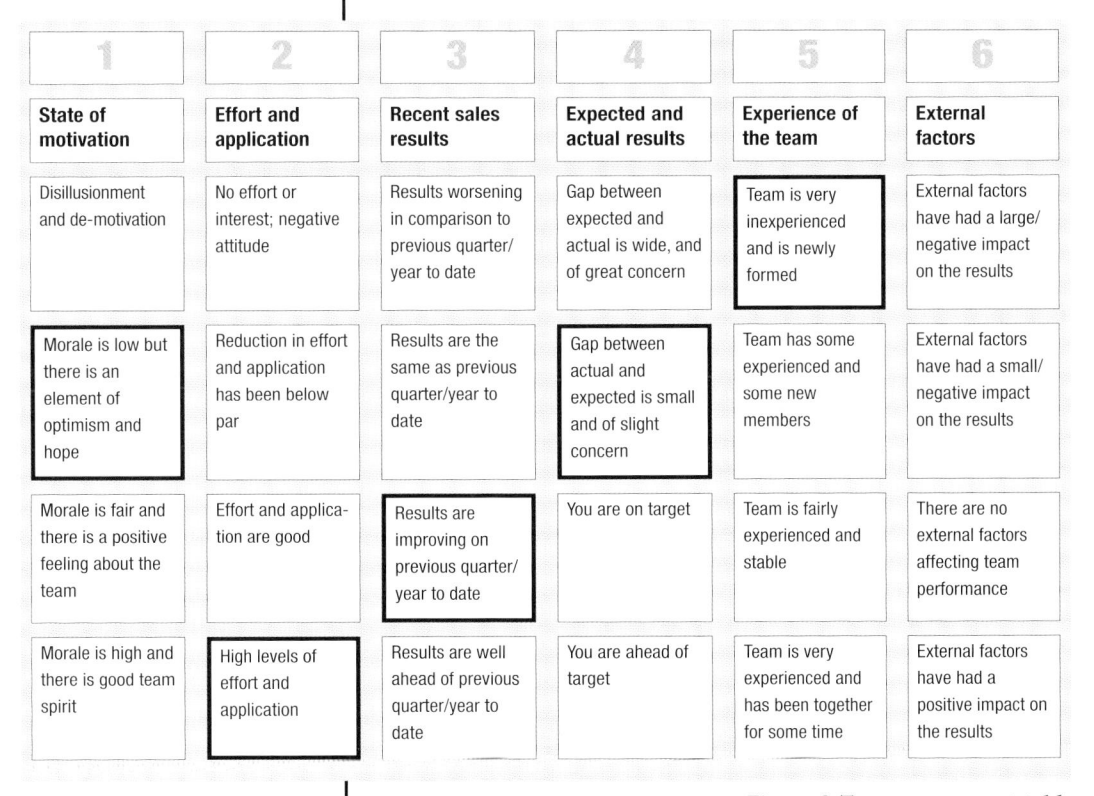

1	2	3	4	5	6
State of motivation	**Effort and application**	**Recent sales results**	**Expected and actual results**	**Experience of the team**	**External factors**
Disillusionment and de-motivation	No effort or interest; negative attitude	Results worsening in comparison to previous quarter/year to date	Gap between expected and actual is wide, and of great concern	**Team is very inexperienced and is newly formed**	External factors have had a large/negative impact on the results
Morale is low but there is an element of optimism and hope	Reduction in effort and application has been below par	Results are the same as previous quarter/year to date	**Gap between actual and expected is small and of slight concern**	Team has some experienced and some new members	External factors have had a small/negative impact on the results
Morale is fair and there is a positive feeling about the team	Effort and application are good	**Results are improving on previous quarter/year to date**	You are on target	Team is fairly experienced and stable	There are no external factors affecting team performance
Morale is high and there is good team spirit	**High levels of effort and application**	Results are well ahead of previous quarter/year to date	You are ahead of target	Team is very experienced and has been together for some time	External factors have had a positive impact on the results

Figure 3: Team assessment table

By reviewing each description the manager builds an objective view of the state of their team. This can help them to select a leadership style, that they believe will best suit their purpose.

In this example, a manager might conclude that this is a below average performance from a team that has the potential to exceed the sales target.

- Morale is fair
- The correct effort is being shown and results are moving in the right direction
- The gap between actual and expected is still of concern
- The low maturity of the team requires strong leadership.

The sales manager might select a Supportive – Forcing style, recognising the team's efforts and pointing out that results are moving in the right direction. An increase in effort and the setting up of specific objectives are needed to achieve this.

- The Supportive element takes into account the effort being shown
- The Forcing element focuses the team on the challenge ahead.

A sales manager must be sensitive to the level of motivation within the team. At times this can be difficult to assess. An objective analysis of the situation can help you to decide on the correct course of action.

Delegation

A measure of the effectiveness of your leadership style will also be reflected in your ability to develop your sales people. Delegating certain tasks will form an essential part of this and will have the following benefits:

- Motivating the team (by helping to make them more effective)
- Developing leadership skills
- Getting the team to interpret your company's strategic goals
- Helping them to fulfil their role as a team member and take responsibility.

Delegation can be defined as giving someone the authority and responsibility to complete a task or action. This will be a time saving for you so that you can concentrate on managing the task rather than actually doing it.

As we have mentioned, delegating some managerial tasks can provide an opportunity for personal development. However, people should not be given so much to do that:

1. It stops them performing their primary sales role
2. It stops you from performing yours.

When to delegate to someone, and how much to give them, are therefore important factors in this decision.

How to delegate

Delegating tasks to people can create more work to begin with, as many tasks need regular review. Questions may be fed back to you and this will require more of your time.

Therefore, in order to build your confidence and to delegate effectively, consider the following points:

1. Ensure that you delegate tasks that provide an element of decision-making and responsibility.
2. Where possible allow the individual to decide how they will implement the task. This encourages initiative and self-confidence.
3. Avoid giving tasks that might de-motivate someone. This could mean that they avoid doing them in the future.

The following steps can help you to decide whom to delegate responsibility to:

Step 1

Select an individual who will benefit from a combination of:

- Gaining experience.
- Improving their leadership skills.
- Adding an interesting challenge to their job.

Step 2

- Ensure that you explain the task fully, including why you are delegating it to the individual.
- Discuss the importance of the task and how it will develop the person. The aim is to motivate them to do it.

Step 3

- Focus on the anticipated results and state that you require a deadline for the task to be completed.
- Decide whether to explain how a task was dealt with on a previous occasion. You can also use the opportunity to encourage the person to suggest their own plan of action.
- Let the individual get on with the task and encourage them to take the initiative.

Step 4

- Plan a way to monitor the individual's progress.

Step 5

- Emphasise your availability to provide help and support when your sales people need it. This can be done by agreeing specific times in the day (or during the week) when you will be available for questions.

Your focus should be on providing support, not apportioning blame. Your role is to resolve problems and to reinforce success with praise.

Leadership

Different ways of delegating

How you monitor a task will depend on:

- The nature of the task
- The individual's level of experience
- Your preferred leadership style.

There are four ways to decide how to delegate a task. These are:

Option 1
We discuss – We decide – You act – You report back

Option 2
You decide – We discuss – You act – You report back

Option 3
You decide – You act – You report back – We discuss

Option 4
Your task – You report back as agreed

The above options give you the opportunity to plan the delegation steps appropriately. They allow you to increase the individual's level of delegated responsibility, depending on their experience, ability and success.

As someone becomes more proficient you can move from Option 1 through to Option 4. As their level of control increases so will their confidence. This provides a valuable learning opportunity for them in a leadership role. It also helps that person to accept a level of responsibility so that you are not doing their job for them!

A sales manager can strengthen the team's motivation and performance by helping sales people to develop themselves in their role. Effective delegation is a good leadership skill for a sales manager to acquire. It requires patience, planning, trust and a good monitoring process.

Chapter summary

In this chapter we have looked at 'Leadership'. This included:

- Understanding leadership
- Leadership styles
- Leading the team
- Delegation.

Effective leadership is about setting clear standards and adapting your approach to suit the differing needs of the individual and the sales team. This requires a sales manager to be objective about their own role and leadership style.

Checklist

✓ Understand the challenges your sales people face.

✓ Focus on principles in line with your personal (and company) standards.

✓ Have a positive attitude.

✓ Be prepared to be flexible in your approach.

✓ Delegate certain tasks (to help sales people develop and take responsibility).

chapter 2

Sales planning

Introduction

A sales manager's plan

Territory planning

Sales targets

Forecasting future sales

Chapter summary

Checklist

Sales planning

Introduction

In order for a sales manager to set standards as a leader he/she will need to have a plan. This will enable them to address the sales issues for the coming year so that the company sales targets are met.

We will now look at:

- What elements are needed in a sales plan
- The importance of giving a sales person the right territory
- Setting targets that are achievable
- The actions needed to predict future sales accurately.

A good sales plan will encourage the correct activity from your sales people. You will then be able to prioritise your time so that you can manage them more effectively.

A sales manager's plan

For any plan to work it has to be understood and accepted by all those concerned. By making your sales team aware of its importance, you will create the right environment for the plan to succeed.

What to put in a plan

A typical plan should address some of the following issues:

- What you want to achieve
- How realistic the plan is
- What measures will be needed to be taken to ensure success
- What could stop the plan working
- Where you start
- Who you share the plan with.

A sales plan will be different depending on your company, your market and your sales objectives. One way of devising a plan is to look at the things you would like to do, or are committed to doing throughout the year. These actions can then be put into the months you would like to do them.

Sales planning

chapter 2

Month	Things to do this year
January	• Break-down sales target and get sales team agreement • Begin 'key' account visits with sales people
February	• Prepare for new product launch • Agree service levels needed for new product
March	• Summer plan with marketing, service and administration departments • New product launch
April	• Review first quarter results • Visit the top ten prospects for new product
May	• Away weekend – sales coaching preparation
June	• Individual meetings with the sales executives to prepare for the 2nd half of the year • Ensure first half year targets are met • Marketing, administration, finance, service conference
July	• Review second quarter results • Sales conference • Plan 2nd half year actions – team sales goals
August	• Help co-ordinate marketing activity of mail campaign
September	• Review of new service levels
October	• Review third quarter results
November	• Meet administration department to discuss year end volume of business
December	• Monitor sales performance versus target for the year
Other items	• Action on poor performers – targeting • Action on top performers – reward/recognition • Regular performance reviews • Regular feedback to sales director

Figure 4: A sales manager's yearly plan

It can be helpful to write things down as this acts as a visual prompt and reminds you of what requires your attention.

Commitment to the plan

By sharing your plan with your sales team, you involve them. This means you are more likely to get their support and commitment. The team may not agree with everything you present. However, if they can see that you have incorporated some of their ideas then you are in a strong position for the plan to work.

A sales manager interprets the strategic direction given by the directors of the company. If a sales person does not agree with key aspects of the plan, then you may want to talk to that person individually.

A useful part of gaining commitment is to encourage your sales people to think about creating a plan for themselves. This might cover aspects of how they aim to reach sales targets throughout the year. It will enable them to look ahead and identify which companies they intend to contact and do business with.

It is one thing to have a plan but another to implement it in a practical way. We often mean to complete a series of actions but find that other issues become a priority. This can affect the plan and some of your original objectives.

Therefore, you should be prepared to adapt and develop your plan, as circumstances change. But if you remain focused on the overall company goals and implement the sales plan properly it will have a positive effect on your sales team. This is because they will see you as someone who can help them achieve results.

Task-related planning

In order to encourage a positive reaction from the sales team; link your plan to a set of tasks. If you do this, it will make your plan easier to understand and monitor. Sales people can easily identify with this because of the nature of their role.

Task-related planning will:

- Make the company's objectives easier to interpret
- Help the sales manager monitor sales people's activity
- Highlight individual activity levels and progress.

Communicating changes to the plan

Good communication is an important part of successful planning. If your plans change they are bound to affect other areas of your company's business.

Remember that other departments will have their own set of plans and priorities. A sales manager should consider sharing a change of his/her plan with other departments in order to get their support.

Sales planning is about setting objectives to meet all of your business goals. It requires discipline and patience. By taking the time to plan your agenda and present it to the team, you will:

- Provide clear direction and leadership to the team
- Enable the team to participate and commit to the plan
- Ensure the plan is implemented properly
- Manage yourself, and your sales people more effectively.

Your confidence will increase as you set a standard for sales performance in order to meet the company objectives.

Territory planning

Giving a sales person a territory that motivates them to want to achieve their targets is a necessary part of the sales manager's planning process. A sales manager needs to spend time defining territories according to:

- His/her strategy (what products and customers are being targeted)
- The potential for existing and new business
- The size of the sales force
- The experience of the sales team.

A territory should be created fairly. Giving someone a sales territory is, in many ways, like giving that person their own business to manage. It is their responsibility to develop it. A sales person must therefore understand what potential that territory has and what is expected of them.

Creating a fair territory

Perhaps one of the most difficult aspects of territory planning is how to create individual areas of responsibility. This can be done in the following ways:

1. By postcode or county
2. By industry sector/vertical markets
3. By distributing existing and new business accounts
4. By the size of company you want to sell into/number of employees
5. By grading the accounts yourself
6. By looking at a company's monthly spend on your range of products.

However the sales manager divides the territory, it must give each individual the belief that they can achieve their target. This will give them a feeling of 'ownership' (of that territory) and motivate them to work on it more effectively. The sales manager will also need to assess each member of the sales team. An inexperienced sales person will not have the same ability to develop certain accounts as someone with a proven track record.

Your company may not have regular opportunities to sell into some accounts. Therefore, you may want to target specific high value accounts. These may be better managed by more experienced sales people. An alternative option is to create a 'major/key accounts' team. This may help to maximise sales opportunities wherever possible.

Changing the territories

Every sales manager will lose members of their sales team when people leave or change roles internally. You will then have to consider finding a replacement. If this happens, one alternative might be to re-distribute an existing territory amongst the remaining sales people.

You may see this as a means of motivating the team as it can save time having to find a replacement, reduce headcount and also reduce overheads. It can also mean higher income opportunities for your existing sales people. However, unless there is a fundamental reason for change, it is rarely effective if the person receiving the new part of a territory is already under-performing. This is because:

- Sales people may find it difficult to properly apportion the extra time and effort
- You may encourage members of your team to lose focus on their existing territory opportunities
- You may be rewarding poor performers for the wrong reasons.

A sales team had four territories, all of which were performing below target. When one sales person left it was decided to distribute that territory between the three other sales people. But it had no effect. Performance actually went down! The sales manager had not properly identified why members of the team were under-performing in the first place.

Ensure that you don't apply one solution to a problem to solve another separate issue! By giving the sales team more responsibility at a time when they were not coping with existing targets, the manager increased the pressure on them. Eventually he recruited a fourth sales person.

Increasing a good performer's territory or customer base can have a positive effect. This will depend on your judgement as to whether the individual can still cover their existing area effectively and cope with the added responsibility.

Taking time to prepare

Planning how to manage a territory must be part of every sales person's responsibility. Sales managers should encourage the team to take the time to prepare themselves and constantly review their actions. This will help them cope with the pressures they may face in their role.

Sales planning

chapter 2

There are two areas to consider when deciding how to manage a sales territory effectively.

1. Information about the **time** it will take to manage. For example:
   - The size/geography of their territory
   - Journey times
   - How many companies they should see in any day, week or month.

2. The **potential of the accounts** on the territory. For example:
   - Which accounts to prioritise on (and grading them to predict their potential)
   - Spending the correct amount of time with an account.

One way of looking at an account's potential is to look at a number of areas:

Grading	Explanation
Size of company	Number of employees, size of offices in UK
Revenue	Turnover of company, potential level of business
Product fit	A company's use of your type of products/service
History	Relationship/expenditure with your competitors
Support levels	Your ability to support a particular account
Profit	Account's ability to invest in your products
Changes	New applications that come about due to future needs

Figure 5: Assessing an accounts potential

A sales manager should also consider:
- The time a sales person spends in the office (compared to on territory)
- Accounts that should be developed with the sales manager's help.

Sales planning

Planning these types of actions in the right accounts is an investment of time for sales people. If a sales manager helps in this process it will ensure that individual territories are managed in the right way. It will help them become more focused on potential areas of business.

A sales manager needs to ensure that sales people have a territory with potential for them to exceed their sales targets. More experienced members of the team should be given more sales responsibility in line with company sales targets.

You should encourage the team to adopt good territory planning disciplines. This will include prioritising their accounts and planning their activity. This will help your sales people manage their territories effectively.

Sales targets

Perhaps the most controversial aspect of any sales manager's role is the setting of sales targets. What can make it difficult is that the company targets may be passed down to the sales manager with little or no consultation. Many companies look for ambitious increases in growth and will set a company revenue and profit target accordingly.

This can put enormous pressure on the sales operation to continually achieve a high level of business. Whether a company target is considered realistic and achievable by the team, is down to the interpretation of the sales manager. You will need to clarify the sales targets and to discuss the sales plan with your own line manager. This should be done before presenting the targets to the sales team.

Breaking down the target

As we have already mentioned, for a target to be realistic, it has to be achievable. The best way of doing this is to break it down into a small set of definable tasks. Then you will present each sales person with something that they can identify with. This will give them the confidence to believe that it can be achieved.

In order to break down a target it is important to consider two aspects:

1. Look at what you **have to achieve** – not what you **think you can achieve**. By doing this you can measure any 'gap' between the two.
2. Ask sales people how they plan to achieve their target.

This will help you to assess whether a sales person's planning is realistic and to compare their planned activity against actual activity in the months ahead. This may alter over the course of a year depending on the results they achieve.

Other benefits of planning and breaking down the target are:

- It gives you a measure of activity
- It gives you a more objective view
- It makes managing the annual target easier.

Individual sales plans

It is not only a sales manager who should consider planning the months ahead. All sales people should be encouraged to do the same.

Once a sales person knows their target they can plan the number of appointments, presentations etc needed to achieve it. This will begin with them making contact with existing customers and potential new ones. Careful planning can avoid sales people wasting time.

Another important benefit to a sales manager is that individual planning encourages sales people to feel more in control of their own territory. They can then assess how their own sales targets need to be met. They can also decide what activity and number of sales will be needed to achieve this.

Quality sales calls

Good planning will help sales people focus on the monthly, quarterly and annual targets. It will also help them assess their ability to work through the stages of the sale in a thorough and professional manner.

Quality sales calls will mean that more activity is spent in the right areas. A sales manager should monitor activity targets set by his/her sales people. This will ensure that they have a clear purpose and direction.

This will:

- Enable you to detect when someone is under achieving at an early stage
- Give you a better chance of correcting the situation.

Many companies are adjusting the way they manage their sales operation. They realise that activity alone will not achieve the results they want. It is the correct focus and quality of any activity that helps determine the level of effectiveness. Therefore, any plan you introduce has to have a level of quality control in it. This will include looking at:

- How sales calls are structured
- What information is being gathered and how is it being used
- What opportunities could be developed.

Attention to detail at the planning stage can help sales people more easily achieve and exceed their sales targets. (We will provide examples of this in Chapter 3 – Managing your accounts – Call plan management.)

By breaking down targets into definable actions it is easier to see how they can be achieved. Sales people should be encouraged to take their time to help them maintain the quality of their work. They should also plan how they propose to meet their sales target. Since this process requires a sales person to identify and overcome challenges, it will increase his/her's confidence and level of commitment.

Sales planning

chapter 2

Forecasting future sales

Forecasting sales is an integral part of business planning. This is because the more accurately you can predict future sales, the more chance there is of a business plan working. This can have a great impact when a company tries to anticipate the demand for their product/services.

There are a number of factors that affect the accuracy of forecasting future business. We will deal with these individually. An essential part of this will be to ensure that sales people see the benefits of any forecasting model. All levels of management in a company will need to discuss how this can be achieved and then implemented. This is not the role of the sales manager alone.

Setting the scene

The importance of forecasting as part of the planning process can be underestimated. The ability to improve forecasting accuracy will help a sales manager to:

- Encourage each sales person to be more objective about their business potential
- Understand the likely level of business coming in every month
- Help sales people manage themselves better as they gain more understanding of how well they are developing the sale
- Look at the actions that a sales person is taking when they are in the closing stages of a sale.

There is a direct link between developing a sale properly and forecasting a sale accurately.

A poor performing sales person is unlikely to want to improve their level of forecasting accuracy if it shows that they are unlikely to meet their target!

Therefore, any introduction of a forecasting model needs to be introduced in a sensitive way. A sales manager can encourage honest feedback from the sales team if he/she can demonstrate how it will help them to reach or exceed target.

Sales people must be encouraged to look at the steps that a buyer will go through at the closing stages of a sale. This way they will find it easier to:

- Define timescales for an order – to produce more accurate forecasts
- Focus on the correct actions to close the sale.

Accurate forecasting becomes easier to achieve if you invest the time to show them what is involved and why it is important.

Challenges involved in forecasting

A sales manager will need to look at a number of issues that will affect the accuracy of a forecast. These include:

1. The balance between optimism and realism (when closing a sale)
2. Communication and contact with different managerial levels (of the buyer's company)
3. Short selling timeframes (a matter of days) or repeat business can make accurate forecasting difficult to predict
4. Sales people may be unaware of the steps involved in making a forecast.

You will need to determine how you can sell the benefits of any change in the way your sales people forecast new business opportunities. Try to assess the level of ability in your team and what areas could be improved. The benefits to a sales person of forecasting future business accurately are that it will be easier to:

1. Plan future business
2. Prioritise on which accounts to focus on
3. Predict sales more accurately
4. Manage the sale better (by having a better understanding of what a buyer is/isn't focusing on as a sale comes to a close).

By looking at these issues you can assess what actions (in the latter stages of a sale) your sales people do well and what needs improvement. Companies' products and selling cycles will differ. Your forecasting model should be designed to reflect a buyer's issues in your particular market.

For any forecasting model to work:

- See it as relevant
- Understand the benefits
- Input accurate information.

The way you introduce a new model is as important as the content of the model itself.

Creating a forecasting model

Where a sales manager decides to create a forecasting model to predict future sales he/she will need to:

1. List the prospect's buying criteria and ensure your product/service matches their need
2. Ensure that all 'key players' involved in the buying process in the account, have confirmed the same timeframe
3. Understand the stages that the prospect is going through as the sale is closed
4. Identify which accounts are likely to produce the most business
5. Confirm the prospect's budget
6. Define a worse, average and best case scenario of what an outcome might be (and attach a percentage forecast prediction to this).

If you currently have a system that uses a percentage to measure success, then try and make this percentage relate to something specific. For example, an 80%+ chance of success means that the sales person has confirmation from the decision-maker that:

- The close date is accurate
- Your product/service matches the prospects need
- Their budget will be spent within a confirmed timeframe
- They are confident that all presentation and pricing issues have been solved
- That your solution is preferred to that of any competitors.

The idea of creating a forecasting model is to also help manage your customer's expectations after they place an order with your company. This is applicable whether your sales people are selling a product, service or both.

Inaccurate forecasting can mean that customers may not receive their product/service when they expected. This can cause them frustration and it can also put pressure on your sales people at the very time they should be celebrating their success.

Short-term and long-term forecasting

For the purpose of this section, a timeframe of one month will be used to describe short-term forecasting. For long-term forecasting we will assume three-six months ahead.

It is harder to predict longer-term business because not all sales issues will have been discussed or resolved. These become clearer as the sale progresses.

It is still important to find long-term prospects so that your sales people have an opportunity to influence their buying criteria. This might include:

- Budget
- Decision-making process
- Application
- Relationship with the competition
- Impression of your product/service
- Timeframe.

For any forecasting model to work properly it must have a confirmed timeframe.

Without specifying this, sales people may have prospects that appear on the list month after month. This implies a lack of knowledge of the account or a lack of certainty surrounding the sale. A sales manager should be aware of this happening, or it will make it more difficult to predict sales accurately

The accuracy of the timeframe can be affected by:

1. A sales person not qualifying the needs of the prospect properly
2. A sales person not understanding the prospect's buying cycle
3. A prospect's circumstances changing
4. A buyer not knowing of any changes to his/her company that could affect the decision to go ahead with the sale
5. A buyer not being aware of his/her own manager's change of priorities.

Factors affecting the prospect's timeframe should be taken into account when forecast predictions are made.

The ability to predict future sales accurately can have other direct benefits for the sales operation as well as the company. These include:

- Increasing the team's confidence
- A more focused sales team
- A greater understanding on how to manage a sales team

Sales planning

- Reduced inventory costs and improved lead times (if you sell an invisible product i.e. a financial service)
- Planning business in a more structured way.

It also gives a sales manager a greater insight into the strengths and weaknesses of each sales person's ability to close a sale properly.

Accurate forecasting is about planning how to manage the stages of a sale. The closer to the end of a sale, the more important a high degree of accuracy becomes. A sales person can list the stages involved in the sale and compare *where they are, with where they need to be*. This can help to prioritise which accounts to develop. It will also help a sales manager produce a more realistic forecast to input into future company sales plans.

Chapter summary

In this chapter we have looked at 'Sales planning'. This included:

- A sales manager's plan
- Territory planning
- Sales targets
- Forecasting future sales.

Good planning will help to develop objectives into realistic actions for sales people to follow. They are more likely to exceed a target when they plan how this can be achieved.

Sales planning

chapter 2

Checklist

✓ Develop a plan and communicate it to your sales people.

✓ Implement the plan and be prepared to review it and develop it further.

✓ Match a territory to a sales person's experience and capability.

✓ Ensure that a sales target is achievable.

✓ Encourage your sales people to know the benefits of accurate forecasting.

chapter 3

Managing your accounts

Introduction

Understanding account management

Call plan management

Applying account management skills

Chapter summary

Checklist

Introduction

Another aspect of a sales manager's role that requires good planning is the development of business relationships. Good account management can lead to profitable business for your sales team.

We will now look at:

- The issues involved in being a good account manager
- The importance of planning a sales call properly
- How you can help your sales team become better account managers.

Sales people need to understand about the companies they intend to sell to. By learning more about the buying criteria and priorities of an account, the selling process becomes easier.

Understanding account management

How to grow your business

There are four main ways to grow a business. These are to increase:

1. The number of customers you have
2. How much they spend
3. How often they buy
4. The effectiveness of your selling (and personnel).

Account management is a key area for all sales managers to achieve growth. In order to sell more to your competitors' accounts, a company may need to build business relationships with different levels of management.

If your sales people develop and manage their accounts well, there is more chance of them keeping that account for many years. Taking the time to understand an account's needs can help your sales people achieve this.

Definition of a customer, prospect and suspect

In order to ensure that sales people understand the different types of buyer in an account, we should define them. There can be a tendency to refer to everyone as a customer. This is unlikely to be true and can complicate the sales process because every buyer will have different levels of:

- Desire
- Purchasing power
- Commitment to a timeframe.

Therefore, this will affect the way they deal with your company and its products/services. This is because the status of certain buyers in an account will be different. This will affect their attitude to your company's products and their desire to buy.

There are generally three types of account. These include:

1. A **Customer** – Someone who is currently using your company's products/services.

2. A **Prospect** – Someone who has actually confirmed that they are looking to buy a product or service within a given time period, from you or a competitor. This would normally be up to six months (depending on how long your sales cycle is). *A prospect can also be an existing customer*, looking for additional/alternative products or services!

3. A **Suspect** – Someone who is not currently in the market but may be at some point in the future. They have not confirmed an intention to buy and have not agreed a timeframe for doing so. A suspect may be interested in your products/services but no agreement to buy from you or from a competitor has been given.

It is important to define which of the above three terms apply to an account you are selling to. For example, their main area of focus could be on product application, value for money or service. They will not then sell to the three above types in the same way. This will help them to think more about what sales strategy to adopt and how to implement it.

(For the purposes of this book, we will refer to the accounts that your sales people want to sell to as **prospects**. This will stop us having to distinguish between the three categories mentioned above in subsequent chapters).

Background information on an account

Some of the information your sales people will need to find out about in an account might include the company's:

- Products and services
- Company history
- Competitors
- Turnover and profit
- Current challenges
- Core business objectives
- Strategic direction
- Company structure.

Most of the information listed above can be sourced from:

1. A company's annual report
2. A company's sales literature
3. A company's web site.

It may take time to learn about your target accounts, but it can help your sales team to develop a good understanding of an account's status.

A company annual report and accounts will give a greater insight into their products, services and most importantly – their culture! It will help your sales people to understand how much value they put on the products and services you sell.

Your sales people also need to have a strategy.

This may be a plan based on the strengths and weaknesses in an account. It may also look at what opportunities you have to develop the account. It should also consider what threats are posed from within the account (personnel, attitudes) and from your competitors.

A SWOT analysis can help your sales people plan a successful strategy because it encourages them to look at the account in an objective way and be well prepared.

Quarterly planning

Another aspect of good account management is to plan ahead and track prospects. As you get nearer the point of selling your product or service to an account, it is important to focus on the right activity needed to close the sale (as we discussed in Chapter 2 – Sales planning – Forecasting future sales). A sales manager can introduce the discipline of maintaining a prospect list that will help the sales team achieve this.

For example, the type of information that sales people can prepare to produce a quarterly prospect includes:

1. The company name and location
2. Their key contact/contacts
3. Which of your products/services the prospect is in the market for
4. The product value
5. Follow up actions needed to progress the sale.

A prospect list can include many accounts, but for this exercise we will only list five (see over).

Managing your accounts

chapter 3

MOST WANTED ACCOUNTS					John Spencer
3rd Quarter					*London South*

Company name and location	Key contact	Prospect for	Value £	Next contact	Follow-up actions
1. Lexon Ltd	P Jarvis	S 200	£200	16 July	Check specification fits and contact PJ for budget approval
2. Williamson Inc.	J Jones	2 x S 500	£3,000	22 July	Prepare presentation to project team
3. Aaron Com.	L Angel	S 200	£200	3 August	Ensure service issues have been covered
4. PFQ Ltd	B Harvey	3 x S 300	£1,500	19 August	Introduce our technical specialist to them
5. Sulu Ltd	M Doe	S 300	£500	5 Sept	Invite M Doe to visit other S 300 user
6.					
7.					
8.					
9.					
10.					

Figure 6: A prospect list

You can add more headings but the key is to track the progress of your sales people's top prospects and monitor the contact with them.

Additional information required for a monthly prospect list might include:

1. Negotiating issues
2. Confirmation of the account being happy with your product, service and application
3. Confirmation of your status as the preferred supplier
4. A meeting to close the sale with the account's key personnel/decision maker
5. A close date.

The nearer your sales people get to closing the sale, the more emphasis there will be on making sure that your product/service fits the prospect's requirement. The prospect's focus on detail regarding application, price, reliability etc will also increase. Furthermore, your solution now has to be preferred to the competition and accepted. How to close the sale (and the issues involved) then becomes the focal point.

Sales people should get used to putting their prospect lists in writing. This gives them a chance to decide which ones are worth developing. It also gives the sales manager an opportunity to review the range of prospects they have and the relationship with each one. When an account is expected to produce a sale within a month, it is essential that all the actions needed to close the sale have been completed.

An account's buying criteria

It is often a small number of actions done well that make the difference between a sale being won and lost. When a sale is won most sales people will think that they know why. However, if a sale is lost, this can be more difficult. This is because sales people don't always look back objectively and try to really understand where they could have done better.

Sales people should, therefore, study an account's buying criteria. Your competitors probably think that they have as good a product, service and sales organisation as you have. If this is the case, how can your sales people differentiate themselves from their competitors?

Imagine that a prospect actually makes their decision on a number of factors. These might include:

1. Product application
2. Service
3. Price
4. Relationship (with you and your competitors)
5. Speed of delivery and quality (of product or service)
6. History (with you and your competitors)
7. Attitude of your company (and the way the prospect is dealt with).

At the end of the sale, a prospect may choose a company that is stronger than their competitors in only one of the above areas. This may be apparent to the prospect throughout the whole period of the sale, not just at the end. Therefore, a sales manager must encourage sales people to identify and then satisfy the prospect's buying criteria at all times during the sale.

A sales person needs to ask the right questions in order to achieve this and to find out the right information. Another element to consider is the sales strategy of your competitors. They will try and persuade the prospect to prioritise on buying criteria, which favours their solution.

It is essential for sales people to focus on the prospect's buying criteria. This has two main benefits:

1. If a prospect's buying criteria does change, sales people are able to see this at an early stage.
2. Sales people will have more time to influence the prospect and ensure that his/her application is best suited to your product and service.

In order to develop better relationships with the companies you want to sell into, your sales team must learn more about them. They should understand:

- A company's buying cycle
- What issues are important to the prospect
- What preferences the prospect has in your product/service related area (and why).

These are important issues for sales people to discuss with their prospects. Furthermore, you and your sales team should track prospects to ensure that the sale of your product or service is being carried out properly.

Later in this chapter we will look at prioritising accounts. This will be a discipline that a sales manager can introduce to focus effort and attention in the right place. The next important stage is to plan the different stages of a call.

Call plan management

Few sales people actually plan a call. Often there is an agenda they want to go through, but it can be vague and not written down. **Every sales call should have a purpose**. Planning a call is important so that sales people are prepared to discuss relevant issues with a prospect and ask the right questions.

It is the sales manager's responsibility to encourage each sales person to plan a call properly. The sales person's approach may be different, depending on:

- How long they have known the prospect
- What sort of person the prospect is
- The history they have in the account
- The prospect's degree of interest.

Good call planning will increase your sales people's chances of developing a sale properly.

Planning a call

Ensure that your sales people think about a number of things before they make a sales call:

About the prospect

1. The level of management they are planning to see.
2. Their job role and area of responsibility.
3. The level of authority and influence they have.

About the sales person's role

1. The purpose of the call.
2. The information they need and what they will do with it.
3. How they can progress a call (and take it to the next stage of the sale).

This can be done on a single sheet of paper and may only take a few minutes. They might also want to grade their questions in terms of importance. This will ensure that sales people seek the most important information first – a particular advantage if they find that their time with the prospect is limited.

For example, a sales person arrived at a prospect's office to be told that their one-hour meeting would have to be cut to 35 minutes. The sales person had not graded the priority of his questions; therefore some of the most important issues were not discussed.

By planning a call, a sales person can decide when to introduce certain topics. This puts him/her in a position to be better prepared to deal with the prospect's questions. This should give the sales person confidence and increase their chances of developing the sale properly.

Managing your accounts

chapter 3

| **CALL PLAN** | **Account manager:** Sarah Jones | **Sales manager:** Robert Brown | **Date:** 14 July |

Company and location	Your prospect's objectives (for your product or service)	Person visiting	Title
NEWTON I.T. SERVICES Oxford	• To develop existing system to make it available to more users – from 25 to 40. • To upgrade XL2 system because of its age (six years old)	James Harris	Systems manager

Existing products or service and from who:

XL2 system – from JDT (new business account)

Proposed products and value:

CR7 system – £4,000 • RG 100 – £260 • 5 x RG 50 – £120 each

Your call objectives/issues to discuss:

- Learn more about their buying criteria
- Gain understanding of competitors proposals/strategy
- Get agreement to see at least two departments who use current systems
- Look at application for new system
- Other departments and personnel involved in the sale
- Time-scale and budget considerations

Your prospect would like:

- To upgrade the current system within three months
- More ongoing training and support
- A better call out time (currently receiving within four hours)

Your prospect must have:

- The ability to upgrade current software
- A system which lasts at least five years
- A faster central intelligence unit

Actions needed to progress the sale:

- Set up a meeting with IT Director – Jane Dyer
- Check upgrade possibilities of our new products
- Set up further meeting with other department heads
- Introduce our systems manager to James Harris

Figure 7: A call plan

The call plan

Once a sales person has decided to make contact with a prospect, he/she should plan the call. A call plan should be simple and easy to understand. This way it will:

- Give the sales person the correct focus. It will allow them to ensure that they cover issues most relevant to the prospect.
- Allow the sales manager to see what members of the team are going to say to their prospect. This can then be measured against what actually happened.

Call plans are useful for every stage of the sale. In the example on the previous page, a sales person determines a prospect's buying criteria.

Purpose of the appointment

A manager will want to ensure that all sales people are making the right type of appointments. Therefore, in order for a sales person to make the most use of their time, he/she should remember:

1. The exact reasons why they are going to visit the person
2. The time they have allowed for the appointment
3. To be flexible and adaptable in their approach
4. Keep it simple
5. To distinguish between what a prospect 'would like' and 'must have'.

One of the main reasons why appointments with prospects go wrong is that the last point is not adhered to. Also, a sales person's questioning is often used to gather information, which may not fit in with the prospect's real needs.

People generally don't buy on what they would like to have, but on what they must have. By understanding this, a sales person stands a better chance of obtaining the right information and of using it to develop the sale.

Your company's sales people are unlikely to be the only ones trying to sell to a prospect in an account. It is therefore important that they are seen as professional, informed and prepared. It is also important that they listen to the prospect's answers carefully in order to understand how to develop the call in the correct manner.

A good sales call will provide relevant information that will help a sales person progress the sale. It will also help the sales manager. This can be done by reviewing a call with a sales person and comparing it to his/her call plan.

Applying account management skills

At various times, sales managers will face a number of common challenges relating to their team's performance and the accounts they manage. The following questions represent some of these. Are you:

1. Winning enough business with competitor accounts?
2. Losing any of your largest, existing accounts?
3. Meeting the company sales targets
4. Developing your sales team properly?
5. Giving your sales team the confidence to achieve greater results?

The solution to some of these issues can be to have an effective method of developing your team's account management skills. This will take time and effort and will require your team to think ahead. You can help sales people to develop this skill.

Benefits of good account management

Breaking into, developing and maintaining an account involves hard work. The benefit of good account management is that it:

1. Shows your sales people how to develop business relationships
2. Enables them to understand how a company actually thinks
3. Increases the confidence of the sales team
4. Maximises on the time available

5. Encourages your sales team to identify how to stay ahead of the competition
6. Sets a standard for developing an account properly
7. Focuses on winning profitable business.

We have looked at some of the challenges involved in becoming a good account manager and the benefits of doing so. Let us now look at what actions your sales people can take in order to develop an account.

Have a sales model or plan to help you

The type of model you decide to introduce will need to address the following points:

- An objective view of what is *actually* happening to an account
- How a sales person can monitor their progress and look to shorten the sales cycle.

An analysis of where you are positioned in an account will help. This should include sales people looking at:

1. The priority of the account
2. The relationship you have at different managerial levels
3. The key players and the decision-maker in the account
4. Future business potential, not just relying on historical data or past relationships
5. The challenges that are faced and the solutions to overcome them
6. The business potential and status of the account – (existing customer or not?)
7. The prospect's buying cycle and decision-making process
8. Where your competitors are in the sales cycle
9. Information/actions needed in order to progress the sale
10. Any current problems/issues in the account and how to solve them.

A good account management model can help determine the type of company your sales people should be doing business with. This will influence them in developing new accounts.

Prioritising accounts

It is better to encourage sales people to develop accounts where they can maximise their selling potential. This is likely to occur when:

- Your company has a good history with the account
- Your sales people have a good relationship with the decision maker
- You have a good application/product fit
- Your level of service matches the accounts need
- Your pricing structure represents value for money.

When sales people determine that one or more of these criteria is met, they can focus on how to develop it. Where a competitor holds an advantage they will need to assess the opportunity for account development.

By taking the time to profile accounts your sales people will:

- Save time in the long-term
- Be more aware of the challenges in an account at an early stage
- Focus on accounts that will produce the most business
- Spend time maintaining the most profitable accounts.

A recent customer care survey showed that it can be six times more costly to attract a new customer than to keep an existing one. Keeping a profitable customer should, therefore, be top of any company's agenda.

By looking at your sales team's account management skills you will be able to assess their ability to handle more complex sales situations. You will also be able to discuss an account with someone individually in a more objective way. This can be done by breaking down actions so that the task of managing an account becomes easier.

Managing your accounts

chapter 3

A good account management model should help a sales manager to effectively develop the team's skills. As more companies are competing for the same business a sales team needs to continually find a competitive edge. By breaking down actions into measurable criteria this becomes easier to achieve.

Chapter summary

In this chapter we have looked at 'Managing your accounts'. This included:

- Understanding account management
- Call plan management
- Applying account management skills.

It is important to give your team a lead so that they know which accounts you want them to develop and what areas you would like them to focus on.

Good account management will help you to build successful business relationships in order to win more sales. It should therefore play a key role in your company's customer relationship management strategy.

Checklist

✓ Good account management needs a strategy and takes time.

✓ Review and be prepared to modify your account management model.

✓ Remember to break down complex tasks into definable actions.

✓ Ensure that a call plan looks at developing the sale.

chapter 4

Building business relationships

Introduction

Managing at all levels

Focusing on the customer

Chapter summary

Checklist

Introduction

We have dealt with some of the practical aspects of account management that a sales manager can introduce. One important element we highlighted was the need to take the time to develop a business relationship in an account.

In order to do this will now look at:

- The people involved in an account's buying process
- The information needed to develop an account properly
- The importance of customer satisfaction.

A better understanding of the people who influence the buying process in an account (and how your sales people deal with them) can often be the key to winning it.

Managing at all levels

Many people in an account can influence what happens to your company's future business. This can include, for example, a marketing manager, a finance director or an IT specialist. As we have stated, your sales people need to take the time to find out about the account they are managing. Other factors to be aware of include the account's:

- Products
- Structure
- Buying cycle
- Attitude
- Competitors.

Sales people will also want to understand the amount of influence a prospect has in an account. In order to do this, they will need to determine which 'key players' are involved (in the buying process) and what level of responsibility they have.

Different levels of management

A sales manager should encourage the sales team to develop a business relationship at three different levels in important/large accounts. The three levels are:

1. **Senior management.** These are directors who run the company and they are more concerned with *strategy*.

    Senior managers are often the ultimate decision-makers. Introducing one of your directors to the account might help the sale. Normally a senior manager will favour this approach if the value of your solution is high and it can be linked to a strategic issue.

2. **Middle management.** These managers normally report to the directors of the company (although in large organisations there can be other layers of management in between). They are responsible for *interpreting* the strategy.

    Some examples of a middle manager might be a marketing, administration or service manager. They are likely to be the budget holders of any proposed spending plans. They are also likely to recommend a sales solution to the directors of their company.

3. **Influencers.** These will be people responsible for the day-to-day *implementation* of the company's strategy. Although they are generally not called managers in title, they are contributing to a vital part of the business. They are the people in the marketing, administration, sales and finance departments' etc.

The approach your sales team might take with an account will depend on a number of factors. These include:

- How well a sales person knows the account
- Whether they are an existing customer.

In a new account it can be better to start at the top and work down.

If a relevant senior manager likes the idea of doing business with your company it can help to build a successful long-term relationship. This is because of that person's:

- Level of influence/responsibility
- Ability to veto a sales proposal (if a budget holder reports directly to them)
- Knowledge of future spending plans (that a budget holder may be unaware of).

However, unless the value of the product/service is high, it is probable that middle managers will have the control of their own budget. They may see a sales person's desire to involve a senior manager as unnecessary or threatening.

Therefore, your sales people should decide:

- Whether to involve senior management
- When to involve senior management
- How to involve senior management.

Company A was the preferred supplier to an account. This was due to a strong relationship the salesperson had developed with a middle manager (budget holder) in the account. When Company B tried to introduce a very similar product at very competitive prices the middle manager showed no interest. He admitted that he had known the sales person at Company A for many years and favoured them because of this.

The sales person in Company B did not want to upset the middle manager. But, by doing nothing there would be no opportunities for short-term future business potential. A course of action might be to try and begin a dialogue between both sets of directors involving the middle manager and the sales person.

Benefits of having different contacts

There are times when sales people should not involve the middle and senior management of their own company in a sale. This might be if it means:

- Reducing the chances of improving the business relationship in an account
- That the sales person is getting a manager to do their job role for them.

It may not be possible to involve every level of management when trying to sell to an account. If you can link your product/service to your prospect's strategy, your sales team have a good reason to begin a dialogue at a senior level. This may gain your company some influence in a future sale.

It is often the middle management level that influences whether your company succeeds in an account. If this is the case, a salesperson will need to know how the departments involved in buying their product/service, interact with each other. This will help your team sell to different people, but with a common goal and understanding of the account's internal structure.

Different types of contact

Many sales people take the time to get to know:

1. The budget holder
2. The person who actually uses the product or service.

This can be enough to win business on a regular basis. However, there are times, especially with larger value sales, when this may not be enough. Other people can be involved but may not have a need to begin a dialogue with the sales person. Or they may not be involved until a later stage in the sale.

Sales people often discover who the 'key players' are in a sale when they lose an order. In order to ensure that they know this information at the beginning of a sale, they should try and find out:

- Who the budget holder reports to
- Which other people may get involved in the sale later on
- How 'key players' in the account interact with each other
- If an account benefits from their own management's involvement
- What other information they need to have (in order to develop the sale)
- Which influencer's have not been identified or met (and their roles)
- Who seems to hold the real influence.

They should make a list of all possible relevant contacts that have and have not yet been met. This can be done with a simple organisation chart:

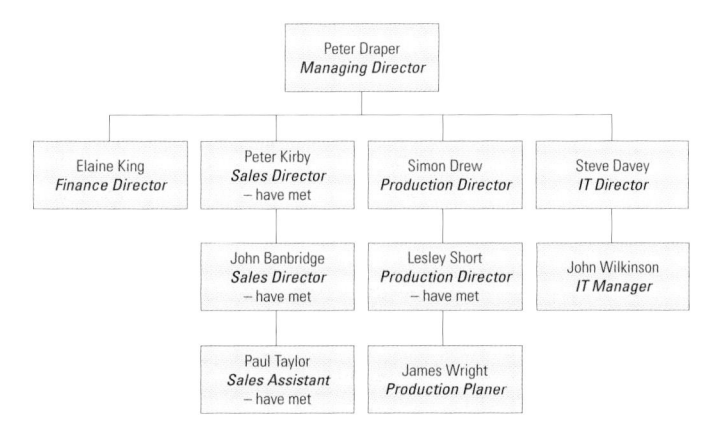

```
                        Peter Draper
                      Managing Director
     ┌──────────────┬──────────────┬──────────────┐
  Elaine King    Peter Kirby    Simon Drew     Steve Davey
Finance Director Sales Director Production Director IT Director
                 – have met
                      │                │              │
                 John Banbridge   Lesley Short    John Wilkinson
                 Sales Director   Production Director  IT Manager
                 – have met       – have met
                      │                │
                 Paul Taylor      James Wright
                 Sales Assistant  Production Planer
                 – have met
```

Figure 8: Johannsen Inc. Organisation Chart

By looking at the level of contact in more detail it is easier to be more objective about where your sales people *really* are in an account. It will also help them to plan a strategy to win the account and they will also be able to decide very early in the sale whether to introduce you or a director from your company to the account.

Communication with internal departments

Your sales people will also need to communicate with different people in other departments of your own company. These departments will have their own plans and ways of interacting with members of your sales team and customers. This interaction will determine the type of relationship they have with your sales operation.

Different parts of your company should be encouraged to communicate any plans that affect your sales team. This will reassure those departments that you are giving them active support.

Sales people will become better 'account managers' if they understand the real needs of their prospects. They will need to know how someone interacts with other colleagues who might affect the buying process. There may be several people who influence a sale. These people are not always those who hold the budget or who have the application for your company's product.

Once this is understood it becomes easier to penetrate an account and get to know the main decision-makers and influencers. From this your sales people can study their buying behaviour and have a better understanding of how to link your product/service to the prospect's need.

Focusing on the customer

Another aspect of good account management that is often taken for granted is focusing on the customer. Their needs are paramount and are a key component of forming successful business relationships. In order to achieve this, your sales people will need to maintain a positive attitude.

Monitoring customer satisfaction

Everyone in a company must have a commitment to customer service. This can give you a competitive advantage. In order to create a good standard of customer service, a sales manager will need to ensure that his/her company is set up properly to deliver this. You should have a long-term plan, as part of the sales strategy, to help achieve customer service satisfaction.

Customer focused behaviour can be monitored in two ways:

1. By having product guarantees/service level agreements that the sales and service team understand and work with.

2. Through specified service measures and targets that form part of performance appraisals. (These can also be partially linked to income.)

It is also useful for a sales manager to receive feedback from external customer surveys. In many companies this is provided by a marketing department. This can be combined with internal checks on areas of performance that are a high priority for customers. By putting these in place the sales team will know what they are getting right and what needs to be improved.

Teamwork

If customers are to benefit from doing business with your company, a high level of customer service focus must exist throughout the operation. A sales manager should be a role model for all customers.

How a sales manager manages their team will affect the way they interact with each other and with customers. Teamwork and co-operation are important behavioural elements in sales performance appraisal.

Customer demands have to be prioritised and qualified, as some customers will be more important than others. A sales manager will therefore need to give proper explanation and guidelines to the sales team. This will create a feeling of unity and a consistent approach. This should also apply to a sales support function.

A sales operation needs to see itself as a team dedicated to working together for the benefit of their customers.

One way of helping to achieve this is to organise regular meetings with sales, support and service departments. This ensures constant communication and encourages discussion about resolving customer issues. This can be combined with occasional internal team (and customer) events involving the sales, service and support operation. A sales manager should make teamwork part of their everyday language.

When people can see that a real commitment to service exists at every level, they are likely to adjust their behaviour accordingly.

When a customer thinks that they will be well supported they are more likely to want to do business with a company. Focusing on the customer will make them feel valued.

Chapter summary

In this chapter we have looked at 'Building business relationships'. This included:

- Managing at all levels
- Focusing on the customer.

Some of the disciplines discussed in this chapter should encourage your sales team to understand the importance of developing an account properly. This will increase their chances of selling into an account on a regular basis and over a long period of time.

Checklist

✓ Encourage your sales people to develop multi-level contacts.

✓ It is important to understand who the 'key players' are in an account.

✓ Good customer service is an important part of maintaining business relationships.

chapter 5

Managing the sale

Introduction

Stages of the sales cycle

Analysing the sales behaviour

Monitoring activity and performance

Chapter summary

Checklist

Managing the sale

Introduction

Developing a good business relationship in an account is one part of managing a sale successfully. Another is to study how the different stages of a sale are managed.

We will now look at:

- The benefits of 'breaking down' the stages of your sale cycle
- How sales people can remain more objective during a sale
- Studying activity and performance to help sales development.

This will help you to identify specific areas of strength and weakness in each sales person. You can then provide guidance to your team on how to develop a sale properly.

Stages of the sales cycle

The stages of the sales cycle will differ depending on your market. A sales manager should look at the average time it takes to complete a sale. This will enable you to define your own cycle and analyse whether a sales person is developing each stage properly.

Learn about your own sales cycle

Examples of stages in the sales cycle are:

1. Introduction (by letter/telephone)
2. 1st appointment
3. 2nd and subsequent appointments/meetings
4. Presentation/demonstration of your product and/or service
5. Negotiation
6. Close > decision. Win, lose or delay!

Not only will every industry have it's own sales cycle, but each stage of the sale will have different levels of importance. This is a major consideration later in this chapter when we analyse a sales person's performance.

You should also recognise the stages of your own sales cycle so that your sales people can 'go back' in the cycle if something goes wrong. If this is not done, it may become too late to rectify. This can lead to a sales person using other factors outside their control as the reason for losing the sale.

A manager does not want to blame the loss of a sale on someone personally. However, a sales person should be encouraged to find out *what* went wrong and *why*. This also applies if they win a sale too!

By consistently doing this type of analysis, a sales person can find ways to improve the proportion of sales they win in the future. It will also help them identify poor opportunities early in the sale. This will increase their understanding and confidence.

A sales manager can teach this discipline by focusing the sales person on the point in the cycle where improvement is possible. (See Chapter 6 – Communication and development – Coaching).

Benefits of sales cycle analysis

There are a number of benefits for a sales manager in analysing their own sales cycle. These include:

1. Allowing sales people to 'manage' themselves more effectively
2. Helping someone move from one stage of the sale to another
3. Shortening the sales cycle
4. Increasing the confidence of poor and average performers
5. Copying the behaviour and traits of successful sales people
6. Maximising on the time available
7. Identifying what sales training and coaching needs are required
8. Looking at past performance in order to maximise on existing opportunities.

Whatever your own sales cycle is, write it down and monitor where your individual sales people are in certain 'high profile' accounts. This will enable sales people to be objective about where they are in the sales cycle.

Identifying development areas

In order to analyse someone's performance properly, a sales manager should look at areas where a sales person needs development.

Example

Someone might seem to develop a sale well by getting to the presentation stage of the sales cycle regularly, but fail to secure an order. This might be because their presentation and negotiation skills need improving. But it could also be because a sales person has not developed the sale properly from the beginning.

If someone is presenting a solution too early in the sale, it will create a number of challenges. The answer may be to 'coach-in' behaviour that encourages someone to develop the sale better. A good sales person will normally present a product or service after the prospect has established a genuine need for it.

NB. *It has to be appreciated that some companies present their products early in the sales cycle. You must therefore qualify the expectation you have for a sales person at each stage of the sales cycle.*

Prioritising on your own stages

Another factor to be considered is to prioritise the different stages, as some will be more critical than others.

Upon entering the UK market, an American company carried out research on their sales cycle. This showed that, providing a sale was developed properly, a prospect would normally decide which supplier to use at the presentation stage. As a result, all sales people were highly trained on their presentation skills.

This produced a more focused sales approach. It also helped the company to sell more of their products in a shorter frametime. The company had taken the time to find out what their potential buyers were thinking and what stages of the sales cycle were important to them.

By taking the time to study your own cycle, sales people can learn about the most important stages. This awareness can ensure that they are properly trained and prepared.

If you take the time to look at how your team is performing in detail, this will lead to a good understanding of how sales people develop a sale. This will help you identify areas where they need help. By looking at the type of activity that takes place you can improve the chances of people developing the sale properly.

Analysing sales behaviour

Few sales people are good at every stage in a sale. Some people like to start a sale off, some are good at closing, and others may be good at presenting their product or service. If you can identify which area needs attention it becomes easier to help someone apply the necessary learning points. Additionally, a manager can monitor sales people's behaviour to ensure that they are developing the sale properly at every stage of the sales cycle.

Analysing your own sales cycle

Many sales managers wish that they could 'clone' the performance and behaviour of their best sales people.

In order to achieve this you will need to:

> 1. Analyse past activity and performance to predict future sales
> 2. Study sales behaviour that has been successful
> 3. Identify where sales people *really are* in the sales cycle
> 4. Study statistics to assess strengths/weaknesses of a sales person

A detailed look at these areas will give you information that you can use to improve your sales people's behaviour. This in turn will help them spend more time on the right course of action.

Intuition

One of the best ways of determining whether something is right is through your own intuition. A high degree of communication is non-verbal! Everyone reads body language, whether in person or on the telephone. **If you feel that something is going wrong – it probably is!** It is a good way of your sales people checking their own feelings against what they see and what they have been told.

Another element to this is delaying doing something that has been agreed to in a given timeframe. A sales manager should encourage members of his/her team to come to a decision on a sales issue and take action. This encourages decisiveness and a positive mental attitude from each sales person.

It is natural that some psychology is involved during all stages of a sale. If you or a member of your team is unsure of what to do about making a decision on a sale related issue, intuition may be the most reliable source.

Being pro-active/re-active

In a selling situation it is important to know when to take the initiative and when to delay. That is the difference between being pro-active and re-active. We have to assess which approach to use on a daily basis. This is not always easy. A manager can help sales people learn this skill by looking out for changes in the way they behave during the different stages of a sale.

Let us look at the parameters of pro-active versus re-active. Assume that one of your sales people has been asked to return a prospect's phone call. Here are some possible responses:

Will call back after a week	▶	Will call back after one day	▶	Will call back within four hours	▶	Will call back immediately

Possible responses might depend on:

- What types of sales person he/she is
- How busy that person is at the time
- Who is calling
- The importance of the call
- Why the person has called.

It is important that they think about the priority of the situation before they decide how to deal with it. The timing of a call and the circumstances in an account can lead sales people (and a manager) to react differently.

Also, a sales manager can decide whether to be pro-active or re-active to many internal demands on his/her time. By consciously making this decision you will be able to prioritise you time better. (See Chapter 8 – Personal effectiveness.)

Using the telephone

Another aspect in looking at stages of the sales cycle is the use of the telephone. This is a quick and easy way for sales people to communicate with their accounts. A large amount of discussion with customers, prospects and suspects is best done in this manner.

Where a sales person is trying to develop the sale, they must be careful to assess whether using the telephone is a better use of time than a personal visit. It is often very difficult to develop a sale to a great extent over the telephone. Sales can be won because key stages are given the attention they deserve and face to face meetings with a prospect have taken place.

A sales manager may wish to monitor how sales people are using the telephone and why calls are made. A pattern of behaviour can then be established to identify whether the telephone is being used for the right reasons.

Ensure that your sales people don't confuse the advantages of *using* the telephone with *selling* on the telephone. The table opposite looks at this.

	Advantages of *using* the telephone		Disadvantages of *selling* on the telephone
1	Inexpensive	1	No personal contact
2	It is quick	2	Less chance to develop relationship
3	No face to face selling needed	3	Substitute for face to face selling
4	It is simple	4	Hard to always measure a true reaction
5	It can save time compared to a visit	5	Can encourage the wrong sales behaviour
6	It can help to qualify someone's interest	6	Shows a lack of commitment

Figure 9: Advantages/disadvantages of using and selling on the telephone

Managing the sale

The telephone is best used for making appointments or asking someone for an update on a situation. A sales person may try to sell their product/service on the telephone (when their role is to develop the sale in person). If this happens, a sales manager will need to assess why this is happening. Possible reasons might be:

- Lack of commitment to the sale (or the job)
- Poor training or lack of training
- Fear of rejection
- Time pressure
- An attempt to shorten the sales cycle.

A sales manager will need to resolve each issue separately. A sales person will need to eliminate the use of the telephone as the primary way of selling a product/service.

Therefore, unless you manage a tele-sales team, discourage your people from actually selling on the telephone!

Knowing when to give up in the sale

Everyone commends a sales person who never gives up and who maximises his or her time and effort. But one discipline that a sales manager should encourage people to apply is to distinguish between effort and the correct focus!

Another aspect of a sales manager's role is the ability to see when someone is trying too hard. This might apply to someone who is under performing, has lost their confidence or is under pressure. If a prospect sees this, it can put them off. It can also influence them to look for a price reduction, if they assume that the sales person is desperate for their business.

One aspect of selling that every sales person should learn is – **when to give up!** Help your sales people see the signs of this early in the sale and correct them. That way you can encourage them not to pursue a lost cause.

Managing the sale

chapter 5

Problems and solutions

One way of looking at an account in a more objective manner is to study the problems/challenges a sales person faces. By focusing on these, he/she can then look to find a solution for each one. It is also useful when discussing an account on an individual or group basis.

The table opposite illustrates a problem/solution page with examples of actions a sales person might take to develop a sale properly.

PROBLEMS/CHALLENGES	SOLUTIONS
1 Our application may not fit	1 Need to study requirement in detail
2 Competition has good relationship	2 References and site visit for prospect
3 Is Purchasing Manager the decision-maker	3 Set up meeting next month
4 New service levels not yet confirmed	4 Set date for service level completion
5 No national service coverage	5 Phase implementation of service
6 Their budget has not been confirmed	6 Meet with Finance Manager
7 No set timescale to buy	7 Establish this with decision-maker

Actions needed to progress the sale:

▶ Look closer at their organisation chart to study any 'key players' who are missing

▶ Find out the relationship and attitude of Purchasing and Finance Manager's

▶ Check that we can deliver the level of service that prospect is expecting

▶ Redefine their 'must have' need to ensure our application will fit

▶ Study how competition is anticipating to solve their problems/challenges

Figure 10: A problem/solution page

It is important that the problems/challenges are not only ones that are perceived by a sales person alone. This is because their perception could be wrong. Therefore, this column should include issues that the prospect has actually confirmed.

Every sales situation has its elements of uncertainty and doubt. This problem/solution table will encourage a sales person to find a solution to problems/challenges. It will also give the manager an opportunity to have a discussion about how the sale is being developed.

Other benefits of this approach are that sales people will begin to focus more on genuine sales opportunities. They will also be more likely to take responsibility for managing *all* aspects of the sale. These might have previously required the sales manager's help and involvement.

Sales people need to know what issues are important to a buyer. This will help ensure that they focus on the right actions needed to increase their selling opportunities. Monitoring their own sales behaviour and that of the prospect can save a sales person time. Monitoring a sales person's activity and performance can save a sales manager time. It will also help to direct a sales persons effort in the right areas and get them to focus on a solution to every problem/challenge.

Monitoring activity and performance

Monitoring the team's activity is an integral part of any sales manager's brief. This can be challenging, as all sales people are unlikely to be performing at the same level at any one time.

It is vital to monitor the sales activity compared to the target on a month-by-month basis. This makes it easier to ensure that all members of the sales team are performing up to the required standard.

Performance expectations

Before you monitor the team's performance:

1. Discuss company sales expectations with your line manager
2. Have a breakdown of the annual target by individuals
3. Look at how each sales person aims to achieve the target
4. Review previous performance against the target (to assess the realism of your team's predictions).

Many sales people will be happy to meet, or get close to, 100% of their target. With this in mind, a sales manager might consider increasing sales targets to prepare for any possible shortfall. (See Chapter 2, Sales planning – Sales targets.)

Each team member should agree to reach at least 125% of target. Assess the capability of each sales person so that you can 'load' their target accordingly. Where possible, ensure that this is done with their approval. If the 'stretch' target is not met by a few per cent then the overall target will still be achieved. This approach is designed to motivate not to put pressure on people.

It is important when you are looking at the performance of your team to remain objective. There might be good reasons for sudden increases or decreases in a sales person's performance. These could include:

- A change in demand for your products/services
- The time of the year (in July and August many people are on holiday)
- Morale
- Personal reasons
- A new product/service introduced by you or a competitor.

Managing the sale

chapter 5

If you are aware of these factors, you are more likely to assess a situation correctly and this will put you in a better position to manage the team. When you evaluate a sales person's results, select a long enough period of time to accurately identify trends in their performance. This is ideally between three months and one year. You will need to take into account seasonal changes in your trading year.

It is also essential to remember that:

- **Activity on its own does not equate to good results**
- **Every sales person is different – look for their trends not perfection!**

In the chart overleaf we can review the last six months performance of someone who is ahead of his or her target. The main target is based on the profit margin that the sales person achieves and the number of units sold.

Key sales indicators (per month = 22 working days)	Target sales performance Average per month (over six months)	Individual result Average per month (past six months)	% against target
Revenue target (per month)	£22,000	£27,000	**122%**
Profit target (per month)	£3,500	£4,900	**140%**
Number of new business appointments	10	15	**150%**
Number of on-going appointments	30	25	**83%**
Number of demonstrations	18	21	**116%**
Number of closing appointments	14	16	**114%**
Number of units sold per month	7	10	**142%**

Figure 11: Key sales indicators

83

You need to set your own key sales indicators so that you can compare a sales person's results to them. By identifying the differences between activity and performance you should be able to improve their focus. This will increase the chances of getting the results you are looking for.

Analysing why sales are won and lost

Not everyone will meet the target criteria perfectly. However, look for a trend that can highlight something which needs corrective action. This might include:

- Target activity levels compared to actual activity levels
- The number of appointments with customers compared to new prospects/suspects
- Comparing the number of presentations or closing appointments to orders.

You can also compare these to your knowledge of the sales person's capabilities and decide what needs improvement. **You are looking to assess the quality of someone's work as well as the amount of activity**.

In order to establish a sales person's strengths and weaknesses, look at where they either lost or won previous sales. Identify at what point they *actually* gave up in the sales cycle. To analyse this data you need to have a start date and an end date. This gives a sales person enough time to analyse the development of a sale from the start to the close.

Managing the sale

Let us look at the steps you could take in order to do this:

Step 1

Out of ten prospects at the end of a sales person's first month, look at what happened to each one. Identify at what point they stopped trying to sell your product/service to the prospect.

Step 2

Once the data has been input, it will reveal a comparison between what an individual 'actually' did against what you would have expected. This data should help you to focus people's attention in the right areas. It will encourage each sales person to develop accounts that have the right potential.

Introduction ▶ **First appointment** ▶ **Subsequent appointments** ▶ **Presentation** ▶ **Negotiation** ▶ **Close order**

Sometimes sales people don't develop accounts properly. This might only be seen when they have a high number of prospects resulting in few orders. If this is happening, consider whether someone is:

1. Qualifying the prospect's buying criteria
2. Developing the sale properly
3. Poor at negotiating and closing the sale
4. Poor at presenting
5. Able to differentiate between a 'must have' and a 'would like' prospect.

It can take time to input meaningful data, analyse it, interpret the findings and then make the correct decision as to each individual's coaching/training needs. However, this will help you to understand the reasons behind someone's performance. Once this happens, it is easier to help someone develop an account properly.

By monitoring sales activity and performance, you will be able to learn more about an individual's strengths and weaknesses. You can then help sales people to manage themselves better and correct mistakes *before* buying decisions are made.

Managing the sale

chapter 5

Chapter summary

In this chapter we have looked at 'Managing the sale'. This included:

- Stages of the sales cycle
- Analysing sales behaviour
- Monitoring activity and performance.

The key to any sales manager's success is the ability to manage a sales team effectively. A study of the sales cycle can help you achieve this and win more sales.

Checklist

✓ Set a standard for sales people at the different stages of your sales cycle.

✓ Ensure that a sale is developed properly.

✓ Encourage sales people to present you with solutions to problems/challenges.

✓ Monitor levels of activity and performance.

chapter 6

Communication and development

Introduction

Behavioural styles

Appraisal

Coaching

Chapter summary

Checklist

Communication and development

chapter 6

Introduction

How we communicate with people is a vital part of maintaining good relationships. This applies to colleagues and people in the accounts your team are responsible for.

In this chapter we will look at how sales managers can:

- Adapt behavioural style to influence different types of people
- Link effective appraisal and coaching formats to produce better sales performance
- Deliver feedback to sales people in a way that builds commitment.

This will help sales managers to develop their staff in their role. It will also help sales people to be more conscious of what they (and their sales team) say to different types of people. It will also enable them to improve their own communication skills.

Behavioural styles

We communicate in different ways and our choice of behaviour will affect our level of success. If a sales manager is to influence different team members, he/she will want to look at how they can adapt the way they communicate appropriately.

While our behaviour is flexible, we will often follow a pattern that represents our preferred style of communication. By understanding this we can compare the style we use with different people and adjust our behaviour accordingly. The skills required to do this can also be used to communicate more effectively with customers.

There are four different behavioural styles that we primarily use to communicate with people:

DRIVER behaviour is about getting things done.

A person with this preferred style of behaviour focuses on:

- Taking action and being in control
- Being assertive and forthright
- Keeping communication short and brief

Communication and development

chapter 6

- Strongly influencing decisions
- The 'bigger picture'
- Achieving goals.

PERSUADER behaviour is about feeling appreciated.

A person with this preferred style of behaviour focuses on:

- Getting attention from others
- Being relaxed and sociable (but still in control)
- Getting others to listen to their ideas
- Persuading others to see their point of view
- Self-expression.

RELATER behaviour is about getting on with others.

A person with this preferred style of behaviour focuses on:

- Approval and trusting relationships
- An atmosphere that is friendly and warm
- Seeing another person's point of view
- Discussing issues fully
- Listening and being attentive
- Being supportive and sensitive.

ANALYSER behaviour is about getting things right.

A person with this preferred style of behaviour focuses on:

- Detail and accuracy
- Analysing information
- Time to make decisions
- The task rather than personal communication
- Efficiency and productivity
- Meeting targets and deadlines.

The main focus of each behavioural style can be seen in the chart below:

```
                    Task-focused
                         ↑
        Analyser         │         Driver
        Get it right     │         Get it done
                  ACCURACY│CONTROL
                         │
Introvert ── ASSERTIVENESS ──────── Extrovert
                         │
                RELATIONSHIPS│ATTENTION
        Relater          │         Persuader
        Get on with others│        Feel appreciated
                         │
                         ↓
                    People-focused
```

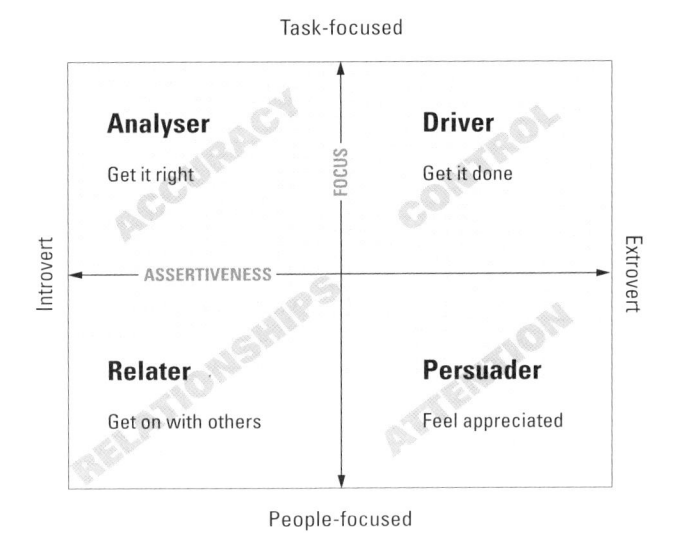

Figure 12: Behavioural chart

Identifying an individual's preferred style is dependent on two factors:

1. Whether the individual is more of an introvert or extrovert
2. Whether the individual is more task-focused or people-focused.

We can have characteristics in all four of these styles. However, it is common to find that each of us will have a primary and secondary style. For example, someone who has a primary style of a 'Driver' may also display traits which focus on accuracy and attention to detail. This secondary behavioural style would, therefore, be that of an 'Analyser'.

When you are looking to influence or build rapport with someone, consider adapting your communication to align with their primary style. Sales managers (and sales people) can determine their own preferred style depending on the type of person they are communicating with. In this way a person you are talking to will:

- Better understand what is being said
- Be more willing to accept your views

Communication and development

chapter 6

- Try harder to have a good rapport with you
- Improve their own communication with you.

It is worth spending time analysing your own behavioural style and comparing it to:

- Individual sales team members
- Colleagues in other internal departments
- Your sales people's customers, prospects and suspects.

This will help you to be more objective about how you communicate with others

Assessing preferred styles

The more we understand about someone's behavioural style, the better the position we are in to influence the relationship. Our ability to respond effectively will also come from our understanding of our own preferred style.

You can determine a person's preferred style using the chart overleaf. Place a mark next to the one that is the closest match to the person whose behaviour you are assessing (as our example illustrates).

Communication and development
chapter 6

CRITERIA	DRIVER	PERSUADER	RELATER	ANALYSER
Appearance:	Business-like Smart	Modern Stylish	Casual Conforming	Formal Conservative
Work area:	Busy Formal Efficient Structured	Disorganised Personal Friendly Untidy	Personal Relaxed Friendly Informal	Structured Organised Functional Formal
Pace:	Fast/decisive	Fast/spontaneous	Slow/easy	Slow/systematic
Priority:	Task Results	Relationships Interaction	Maintaining relationships	Task Process
Under stress:	Dictate Assert	Attack Become defensive	Submit Avoid	Withdraw Avoid
Security from:	Control Leading	Flexibility Being appreciated	Close relationships Being team player	Preparation Correct analysis
Wants to maintain:	Success	Status	Relationships	Credibility
Likes you to be:	To the point	Stimulating	Pleasant	Precise
Wants to be:	In charge	Admired	Liked	Correct
Frustrated by:	Inefficiency Indecision	Boredom Routine	Insensitivity Impatience	Surprises Unpredictability
Measures worth by:	Results Track record Measurable progress	Acknowledgement Recognition Compliments	Compatibility with others Depth of relationships	Precision Accuracy Commitment
Decision making:	Decisive	Spontaneous	Considered	Deliberate
TOTALS	**7**	**2**	**2**	**1**

Figure 13: Behavioural style chart

Interpreting the chart

The column with the highest total suggests this is the person's preferred behavioural style. By knowing this you can adapt your own style to maximise your communication skills.

Below, we have illustrated the different ways of responding to each style:

Driver behaviour

- Be assertive and forthright
- Discuss business first
- Keep to the point and maintain energy and pace
- Give them the opportunity to communicate
- Allow them to get involved in the decision-making process.

Persuader behaviour

- Allow them time to express their opinion
- Have empathy
- Have a clear agenda (as they may not have one)
- Use a relaxed but controlled manner
- Recognise their efforts
- Request their co-operation.

Relater behaviour

- Set up a friendly atmosphere
- Relate to their perception of a situation
- Gently express your own opinion
- Be sensitive and listen to them
- Stress their positive contribution
- Offer support and encouragement.

Analyser behaviour

- Use a structured approach
- Focus on the reasons for the meeting
- Stick to an agenda
- Be logical/rational/use examples to clarify
- Avoid having a personal discussion
- Focus on work-related matters.

The degree of flexibility you use in your own behavioural style will influence how well you communicate with others. Having a flexible approach when you are talking to people is an asset. A sales manager has to talk to many different types of people with very different personalities. A method of being able to improve that communication will give you more chance of developing successful business relationships.

It is not always possible to perfectly match someone's behavioural style. However, a better understanding of the type of person you are dealing with, will give you the opportunity to improve your own communication skills. This type of flexibility and adaptability can be of particular use when appraising individual sales people.

Appraisal

Performance appraisals should form part of an on-going process of review and development. A pro-active plan to support a sales person can be highly motivational. It can also help develop someone in his or her sales role.

In order to achieve this, use an appraisal format that will be easily understood by both you and the sales person. (Most companies have a Human Resources/Personnel department who will have a standard appraisal system.)

If, however, you do not have this facility you may want to create your own. In this section we will develop a format that:

- Monitors sales performance and personal development
- Can be easily understood and implemented

- Provides the sales person with a clear improvement plan and supports their ideas and goals.

In addition, we will look at how to give praise and constructive feedback to someone in a manner that maintains the person's morale and commitment.

Frequent reviews

Ideally, a sales person will need some type of performance appraisal more than once a year. Consistent review of performance is an important element for self-improvement. While appraisals can be lengthy, reviews should be part of a sales manager's 'coaching' plan.

You may want to keep individual records of assessment and progress. Each review will then focus on one or two areas for improvement and specific follow-up actions.

This makes the annual review far more relaxed and up-to-date with less time spent on past performance issues. More time can then be spent on present issues and future goals.

Having a model

The primary focus of any appraisal will be the sales performance compared to the target. This will need to be linked to specific areas for improvement. The table overleaf is an example of a method for appraising an individual's performance and providing a focus for improvement. In order to do this effectively you would need to decide on:

- The assessment categories
- The subject (and the standard required for each one)
- Your evaluation of a person's performance
- What your own perception will be of a poor through to an excellent performance.

Communication and development

chapter 6

Scoring

1 = poor

3 = below standard

5 = average

7 = very good

9 = excellent

Highlight your expected standard against which you can evaluate a person's performance.

SUBJECT	EVALUATION
KNOWLEDGE	
Products	1 3 5 7 9
Customers	1 3 5 7 9
Company	1 3 5 7 9
Competitors	1 3 5 7 9
SKILLS	
Planning/time management	1 3 5 7 9
Quality of appointments	1 3 5 7 9
Presentation skills	1 3 5 7 9
Negotiating/closing the sale	1 3 5 7 9
Letters/proposals	1 3 5 7 9
Assertiveness	1 3 5 7 9
Developing relationships	1 3 5 7 9
Problem solving	1 3 5 7 9
Interpersonal skills	1 3 5 7 9
ATTITUDES	
Positive and enthusiastic	1 3 5 7 9
Helpful and understanding	1 3 5 7 9
Problem solving	1 3 5 7 9
Initiative	1 3 5 7 9
Dress code	1 3 5 7 9

Figure 14: Assessment table

Communication and development

chapter 6

Preparing to use the assessment table

The following ten points explain how to introduce and use the chart as part of a performance appraisal:

Step 1: Ensure that the criteria in the chart relates to the sales function you manage.

Step 2: Highlight the expected standard (score) you require for each of the criteria. You may decide certain criteria carries greater emphasis.

Step 3: Make copies for your line manager, each sales person and yourself.

Step 4: Explain that you would like people to assess themselves by placing a circle around the score that in their judgement represents their level of performance.

Step 5: Explain to each person that the chart is a means of assessing performance gaps. It will determine how best to support their progress and development (and possibly be a factor in deciding on a basic salary increase).

Step 6: State a deadline and arrange specific appointments when you will meet with each person.

Step 7: With your copies, complete a form for each person, placing a circle around the score you would give them for each criteria.

Step 8: Make notes as to why you have selected each score.

Step 9: When you meet with the person, explain that you are looking to help them improve and succeed further.

Step 10: Compare your scoring with theirs for each item. Use the scores to initiate discussion. Concentrate more on the specific issues and areas for improvement rather than the scores themselves.

The aim is to create a benchmark for performance that you and the sales person clearly understand and agree upon. Our scoring format limits choice in order to encourage clear decisions on assessments of performance.

The development/action plan

Another benefit of using an assessment table is that it allows you to set up a personal development plan. Your scorings will determine the areas you may wish to focus on, as in the example below:

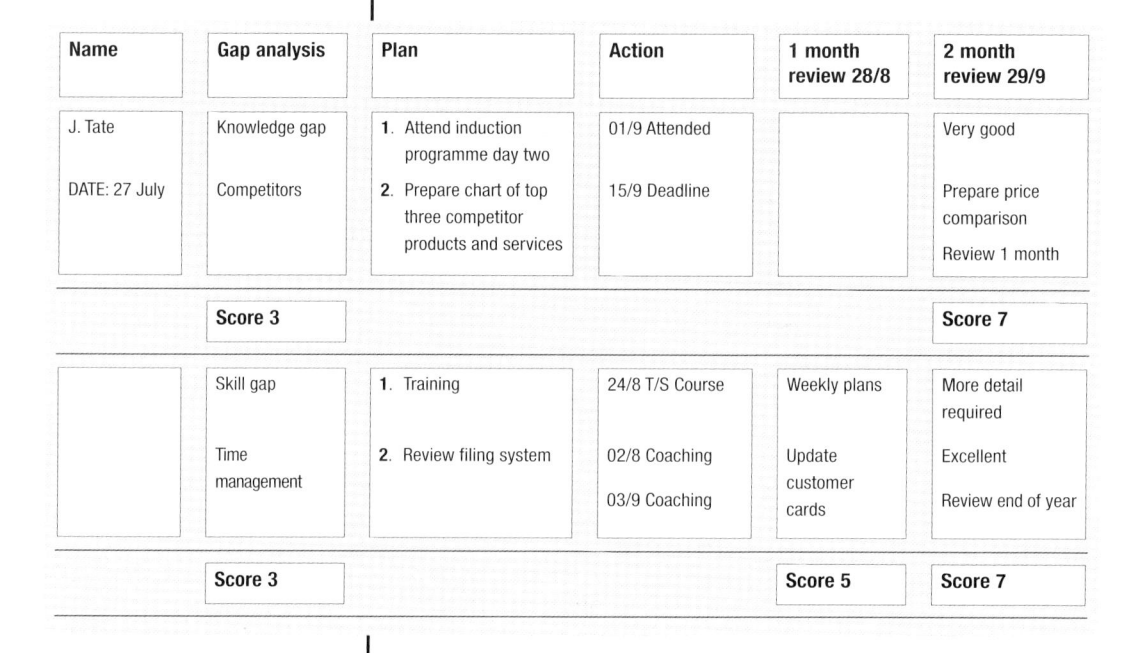

Name	Gap analysis	Plan	Action	1 month review 28/8	2 month review 29/9
J. Tate DATE: 27 July	Knowledge gap Competitors	1. Attend induction programme day two 2. Prepare chart of top three competitor products and services	01/9 Attended 15/9 Deadline		Very good Prepare price comparison Review 1 month
	Score 3				Score 7
	Skill gap Time management	1. Training 2. Review filing system	24/8 T/S Course 02/8 Coaching 03/9 Coaching	Weekly plans Update customer cards	More detail required Excellent Review end of year
	Score 3			Score 5	Score 7

Figure 15: The development/action plan

From our example the following areas represented key performance gaps:

- Competitor knowledge
- Time management.

The above plan looks at how to address these gaps. The sales person can attend an appropriate training course. Specific goals and actions are agreed and supported by individual coaching. By doing this, the learning points become part of the individual's daily routine. This will increase the chances of them being used as part of their everyday behaviour.

The review process

After one month the time management issues are reviewed. The sales person now scores 5. One month later they have demonstrated improvement to achieve a score of 7. Competitor knowledge is also due for review at his point. The sales person achieves an improvement here too, with a score of 7.

The sales manager can now concentrate on another priority in the chart and put a plan in place with the sales person. This may involve other initiatives – coaching, training, project work, time with an experienced sales person etc.

A copy should be held by you and by each salesperson and items updated accordingly. That way you can both monitor progress and follow-up actions can be noted.

Giving feedback and praise

When sales people receive recognition from their sales manager it can be highly motivational. Feedback on past and current performance can also be handled in a manner that produces a positive desire to improve.

Where possible a sales manager should give feedback in a relaxed and friendly manner. Try to avoid using words that could cause the person to take a remark out of context. This reduces the chances of any comment being taken personally.

Additionally, when you feedback corrective comments, include positive points about the individual's performance. This can lower defensiveness and create a more balanced feel to the interview.

Someone being given feedback may not wish to confront an issue and may avoid taking responsibility for it. You should, therefore, respond with empathy and try to understand the other person's point of view. But, in turn, they must be willing to commit themselves to an agreed corrective action. (If someone becomes defensive or lacks motivation, consider coming back to the issue at a later stage or ask them if this particular issue worries them.)

Communication and development

chapter 6

Everyone likes to receive praise for doing something well. When giving praise, be positive and sincere and have direct eye contact with the person. Discuss the area you are particularly pleased with. You can compare a person's level of ability at your last review with their present level.

By doing this you will focus on someone's progress. It will then give you an opportunity to look at other areas you may want them to develop. People are more likely to want to try something if they feel positive about themselves. Praise that is deserved increases confidence and lessens a fear of failure.

One example of how to deliver praise and constructive feedback to team members is through the B-A-R-E-F-O-O-T technique. This provides a sales manager with a structure that encourages full understanding of the issues. This will then promote a better discussion between the sales person and yourself.

B ehaviour **A** ction	Describe the behaviour and actions taken by the individual
R esult **E** ffect	Explain the result of that behaviour and its effect on others, their performance, and operation
F eelings **O** pinion	Share how you personally feel about it Point out positive traits
O ptions **T** hank	Discuss what can be done Thank them for their contribution/co-operation

When you use this technique to give feedback, remember:

*It is not so much **what** you say, but **how** you say it.*

(This is dealt with in more detail in Chapter 7 – Motivating the team.)

Giving constructive feedback

The B-A-R-E-F-O-O-T technique is particularly useful when giving feedback on behaviour that is unacceptable. A more assertive approach may be required and the feedback should be delivered in private. This should avoid you both being distracted, which could cause potential embarrassment to a sales person.

For example, if a sales person is consistently arriving late you might take them to one side and deal with the issue in the following manner:

B ehaviour **A** ction	Point out that the individual has arrived late for the past four days
R esult **E** ffect	Explain that others have noted this and are de-motivated by the sales person's lack of commitment
F eelings **O** pinion	Describe your own concern and frustration as it challenges your authority and contradicts their otherwise positive contribution to the team
O ptions **T** hank	Ask why they have been arriving late and open discussion on how this will be avoided in the future If appropriate thank them for co-operating

Your ability to give feedback in the correct manner will determine how much of a change that person is prepared to make.

Giving praise

The benefit of the B-A-R-E-F-O-O-T technique is that it helps you to give feedback in a more structured way. When giving praise, the 'Options' step can be used to ask the sales person how others in the team might benefit from their particular skill in completing the task.

The example below illustrates how you might praise someone's contribution:

B ehaviour **A** ction	Thank the person for meeting the deadline on the piece of work and for completing it so competently
R esult **E** ffect	Describe how it enabled you to present successfully to senior management and achieve an important decision
F eelings **O** pinion	Describe how pleased you were with the result and how you were impressed with specific aspects of their work, which contributed so positively to the presentation
O ptions **T** hank	Discuss how other team members can learn/benefit from this Thank them again as a final reinforcement

Sales managers are more likely to create the right environment for continuous improvement when they take the time to share their appreciation of someone's good work.

Appraising people can be a difficult process because you are trying to be objective about someone's personal development. Having a format and using it to appraise people is a valuable part of the sales manager's role. How you introduce this and the way you communicate feedback will affect its level of success. It will also determine:

- The respect you get from your sales team
- How well they progress in their role.

Another aspect of helping members of your team develop is to spend time with them discussing 'live' sales issues. This can be through one-to-one 'coaching'.

Communication and development

chapter 6

Coaching

In a sales role, coaching can be defined as teaching, helping, advising and supporting someone. Behaving in this way can help a sales manager to improve a sales person's performance.

To coach someone successfully you will need to focus on specific issues and build a good understanding with the sales person. You will also need to have a structure so that both parties understand:

- What needs to be improved
- Why it needs improvement
- How this will be achieved.

Ideally, this should form part of your appraisal and development plans.

When to coach

The need to coach someone normally takes place when a sales person:

1. Is learning a new task (and time is limited).
2. Needs help to improve their sales performance.
3. Needs help in a particular area (developing an account, improving their sales skills).

Steps to effective coaching

A coaching need may be identified from an appraisal or review. At the beginning of a coaching meeting, ensure that:

- You look at the reasons for the required coaching
- The person accepts the need for it to take place
- You check the sales person's attitude is positive.

Communication and development

The points below will provide you with a structure to follow:

Step 1: Assess the sales person's present performance level
(see Assessment table, page 96)

Step 2: Determine the individual's perceptions and expectations

Step 3: Develop a plan to achieve agreed goals
(see Development plan, page 98)

Step 4: Implement the plan
Encourage the sales person to use the desired behaviour/skill

Step 5: Monitor their performance

Step 6: Give feedback and offer support

A sales manager should ensure that the sales person takes responsibility for learning/developing the skill you are coaching. This will involve encouraging that person to:

- Review their actions
- Make their own suggestions for improvement.

If you want to coach someone effectively, any change has to become part of that person's everyday behaviour. Coaching can be effective, whether people are above or below their target. An experienced sales person will often welcome an objective view of a sales situation from his/her manager.

However, if a sales person's performance is consistently below target a coaching initiative may be needed to ensure that they remain focused and motivated. It will also be useful to ensure that they are behaving in the right way with your customers, prospects and suspects. We can now look at this in more detail.

Dealing with poor performance

With the current demands placed upon sales managers, it is difficult to spend enough quality time with all sales people. A good sales person will set high standards of behaviour and will be professional throughout their daily routines.

However, where individual sales performance is below an acceptable standard, this must be addressed. This is because it could have an effect on your overall team performance as well as that person's morale.

While it is easy to identify a poor performance, it can be difficult to change a person's behaviour in order to produce a higher level of achievement.

A sales manager needs to review the preparation that the company is giving its sales people. This may include:

- Informing them of the company's expectations (in terms of activity/expected performance, before they take on a territory)
- Making them aware of help available to them (how to get it and when to ask for it).

The reasons for a sales person's consistent poor performance need to be understood and monitored by a sales manager. If this is done there is more chance that the correct coaching can take place to help the individual.

What can be the underlying causes for a person's poor performance?

1. They do not feel that they are being given the right support from the company/manager
2. Their sales targets are too high/not enough target accounts
3. They are not properly trained/the wrong person for the role
4. They are working hard but in the wrong areas/not motivated
5. They are unhappy with something in their personal lives that is affecting them at work
6. There are internal problems with the company, its products/service or they fear the competition
7. They do not like their manager or some of their colleagues
8. They are happy supporting themselves on a below average performance/not used to making the required effort.

If you find that someone has lost their ability to function properly in a sales role, there are a number of indicators to look for:

- Absenteeism/poor health
- Poor time keeping
- Lack of enthusiasm
- Disruptive behaviour
- Examples of stress.

A poor sales performer needs help. Try and identify the underlying causes. In order to achieve this you might want to:

1. Talk to the person about it. You will want to find out where they feel the problem lies and get their agreement on how to solve it.
2. Monitor how they are managing the different stages of a sale.
3. Look at the standard of the work they are doing and the type of business they are bringing in:
   - Are they talking to the right people in an organisation?
   - What areas of their work are good/poor?
   - What is their attitude to their poor performance?
4. Devise a training/coaching plan to put them back on a path to success.

If a poor performer continues to under-achieve after a period of support from you, further action will be needed. This will depend on whether you have successfully identified what the underlying causes are.

If you have, then you might consider talking to the sales person about their suitability for the role. If you conclude that they are unsuitable, you will want to involve your own line manager and the personnel department (if you have one). This is a last resort but it is generally better to confront an issue rather than put it off. In many cases, you will be able to identify sales related issues causing poor performance early on and correct them.

Coaching can provide the right type of support to any sales person looking to develop themselves in their role. For it to be successful, a sales manager needs to give feedback and allow time for any changes to take effect.

Taking the time to make a correct analysis of why someone is under-performing will help them to improve. For this to happen, the new behavioural skill needs to be understood by the sales person. Coaching them can achieve this. It must then be practiced so that it becomes part of their everyday routine.

Chapter summary

In this chapter we have looked at 'Communication and development'. This included:

- Behavioural styles
- Appraisal
- Coaching.

Understanding the type of people you deal with and being a good communicator is an important part of being a sales manager. By monitoring a person's sales performance you will be in a better position to appraise them and identify any coaching/training needs. This is an important element of developing people in their sales role.

Checklist

✓ Be aware of your behavioural style (and that of others).

✓ Introduce an appraisal system to help develop your sales people.

✓ Review performance and look for sales development opportunities.

✓ Use coaching sessions to improve a sales person's skills.

chapter 7

Motivating the team

Introduction

An individual's goals

Motivation theory and practice

Influencing behaviour and attitudes

Motivation and reward

Chapter summary

Checklist

Motivating the team

chapter 7

Introduction

How you communicate with and support the sales team will affect the general working atmosphere and the desire to perform. We will now look at how you can further encourage a positive working environment to motivate the team.

We will focus on how you can influence commitment and affect performance by:

- Understanding the needs and personalities of each individual
- Recognising the factors that they respond to most positively
- Improving the tone of your communication
- Introducing different ways of rewarding progress and achievement.

While financial rewards play a key part in raising sales performance, we will look at how these areas can help to produce consistently high results and commitment.

An individual's goals

It is common for a sales manager to talk about '*the sales team*'. It is the performance of the team that will determine your success; the team, of course, is a group of people with individual sales targets.

Achieving and exceeding targets should create a positive feeling in each sales person. But you will also have to consider the different ambitions, desires and goals he/she wants to fulfil at work. These personal goals create expectations and if they are met, that person is more likely to perform well and remain enthusiastic about their role.

A sales person's expectations should match those of your department and those of the company.

Individual and company goals

There are two aspects to a sales person's development in a company:

1. The achievement of sales targets (a financial goal).
2. Personal fulfilment (a subjective set of goals).

Setting up personal development plans can be a positive motivational factor. It is important to encourage sales people to reveal their personal goals to you. These can then be monitored and acted upon alongside the company sales target.

A sales manager can take an objective look at the company, team and individual goals by listing them and noting any marked differences.

For example:

Company goals	Sales manager's goals for their team	Examples of individual goals
To increase profit by 3% next year	To gain at least 10% of new accounts	To meet 150% of annual company target
To increase revenue by 9%	To ensure that all the sales team achieve 100% of their target	To develop bottom ten least profitable accounts
To bring at least two new products into the market	To help at least two team members win a large new account	To be more thorough with internal company paperwork
To reduce the time taken for new products to be built and to then get to market	To be the top sales team in the UK	To prepare for possible major account sales role
To prepare all company personnel for ten year business plan changes	To spend more time with each individual account manager	To spend more time preparing a sales call

Figure 16: Individual and company goals

You can then ensure that a sales person's goals match those of the company. Everyone in a sales team needs to be fully aware of the company's objectives and sales targets to enable you to:

- Build a team strategy that takes these into account
- Manage and monitor company, team and individuals' goals.

In order to maintain someone's level of motivation and enthusiasm you should ensure that they feel a goal is achievable. Also, every person's goals will differ in some way even if their overall sales objectives are the same.

By making an effort to understand your sales people, achieving the targets and managing them becomes easier.

You should treat your sales team as a group of individuals with different needs and different goals. This will help you understand their personal motivation.

It will also:

- Help you become a better team leader
- Improve the quality of your communication
- Increase the team's confidence
- Encourage their desire to perform to the best of their ability.

In order to have a better understanding of what 'drives' sales people, we need to look at the theory of motivation.

Motivation theory and practice

A sales manager can make practical use of the research carried out on the theory of motivation. If you understand what motivates your sales people you can manage them more effectively. There are two important areas of research that provide a means of:

- Developing your understanding of your team
- Creating the self-motivation you seek from individuals.

Motivating the team

chapter 7

1. Maslow's (Hierarchy of needs)

Abraham Maslow, an American-born psychologist, published his 'motivation theory' in 1943, which stated that human beings focused on a hierarchical set of needs. Until the first set of needs were met and satisfied, a person would not move on to the next level.

Level 1: Hunger, thirst, warmth, shelter
Level 2: Security
Level 3: Need to belong
Level 4: Identity, self-esteem
Level 5: Self-fulfilment

While people will operate on a more complex basis than this, there is a practical element to consider. Assess your sales people on these levels and use it as a structure for understanding how they operate. Consider what their personal circumstances and goals are and what they are focused on.

Level 1: Does this person have adequate resources?
- What accommodation do they have?
- Where do they live and with whom?

While their lifestyle may be a personal matter, it can be a relevant factor for you to consider if it affects their sales performance.

Level 2: What is the meaning of security for this individual?
- Buying a home?
- Having a steady stream of income?
- The ability to pay their bills?
- Savings?
- A career?

Level 3: What elements of sociability can you identify?
- Are they a team player?
- Do they seek the company of others?
- Are they responsive to attention from others?
- Is the company culture important to that person?

Level 4: What does this person appear to value most?
- Recognition from others?
- Good sales performance?
- Having strong opinions?
- Being a good negotiator?
- Being seen as a decision-maker?

Level 5: Does the individual have a goal that represents their peak of achievement?
- What do they strive for?
- Do they have high ambitions?
- Do they want to progress in the company?
- Are they happy?

You can identify areas that will help you to understand a sales person's individual personality. You will also be able to look at their level of motivation and whether it is influenced by personal (external) or company (internal) factors.

By stressing a particular value that someone feels strongly about, a manager can reinforce the person's self-worth. This might influence a person's desire to make a positive contribution to the team. As part of their review sessions, ask them what aspects of their role they intend to focus on. This will help you understand what motivates them.

2. Herzberg's (Hygiene and Motivating factors)

According to Fredrick Herzberg (an American clinical psychologist working in the 1950s and 1960s) two separate sets of factors influence human behaviour:

1. The need to avoid pain/obtain the basic necessities of life.
2. The need to develop their own personal capacities/fulfil their potential.

Factors that caused dissatisfaction at work (hygiene or maintenance factors) were often different from those that created satisfaction (motivating factors). Motivators encouraged better quality of work while hygiene factors did not necessarily do this.

Herzberg applied two measures to his model:

1. How long the feeling of satisfaction/dissatisfaction lasted.
2. How intense the feeling was.

His research concluded that:

- A poorly paid job would create a dissatisfaction that was fairly intense and lasted a long time
- A well-paid job would create intense satisfaction for a relatively short period of time.

Therefore, while the level of salary is important, it will not necessarily be the prime motivating factor. This is a valuable point to remember when a sales manager is looking at what motivates team members.

An employee might resign because of an inadequate hygiene factor (such as poor working conditions). But they would not necessarily work harder if it was satisfactory.

Many factors based on self-esteem; recognition and evidence of contribution and progress were found to be the highest motivators. It may be worth noting that the majority of the above motivators do not require more financial outlay. But they require the investment of a manager's time and effort.

The table below indicates the prime de-motivators (hygiene factors) and motivators.

DE-MOTIVATORS	MOTIVATORS
Poor salary	Good salary/commission structure
Redundancy	Security
Not producing results	Interest/progress in their job role
Commission/bonuses reduced	Achievement
Fear of change	A challenge
Inability to cope with role	Job satisfaction
Boredom	Praise for achievement
Frustration	Good team spirit
Poor management	Respect from colleagues
Not being appreciated	A good manager
Lack of recognition	Responsibility – to use abilities
Poor relationship with colleagues	Complaints/suggestions listened to
Lack of information	Opportunity to learn and progress
Inadequate training	Recognition for effort
Lack of career opportunities	Feedback on results/direction

Figure 17: The prime de-motivators and motivators

If you identify a sales person's fears and aspirations in their current role, it will give you an opportunity to address their main concerns and expectations.

Motivating the team

chapter 7

An information technology company dramatically reversed their poor turnover of sales personnel (30% per annum). They achieved this by matching the job role to the candidate during the selection process. Carrying out exit interviews when existing sales people left also helped to identify common de-motivational factors that caused a person to leave. Some of these were:

1. *Frustration with the company work style*
   (not what they had expected)

    Response: Recruit people who would actually enjoy working for them. The focus was placed on assessing the salesperson's 'motivational' suitability to the role by collating information during interviews, as shown below:

Motivational 'fit'

What do they like about selling?	Does it form part of the job?	Key part of job?
Working with a team	Yes – team approach to sales	Yes
Short sales cycle – quick sales	No – long sales cycle	No

What do they dislike about selling?	Does it form part of the job?	Key part of job?
Administration and paperwork	No – support team	No

2. *Salary/benefits not the main issue*

    Response: Keep paying them very well, as this was a condition of being a competitive employer in the market place. It was not the biggest differentiator, but it would help the company avoid losing short-term competitive advantage.

3. Perceived lack of training and career development

Response: Provide regular training opportunities with tailored programmes for all sales roles. Involve experienced sales personnel in helping to train others and provide 'advanced' learning opportunities.

4. Frustration with 'not being able to have enough time to sell'

Response: Create more time for them to sell by reducing tasks (like too much administration) that were de-motivating them. This had caused sales people to spend less time with customers.

By looking at motivational theory a sales manager can understand what motivates every individual in the sales team. Every person will have different needs, fears and aspirations. It is easier to manage someone if you know what these are.

Influencing behaviour and attitudes

In chapter six we stated that understanding your sales people's attitude is a key element in influencing their response to different people. While you can make conscious efforts to match behavioural styles with others, the tone of your communication will affect how successful this is.

In this section we will look at how we can influence other people's behaviour through the tone of our communication.

People notice what attitude we have through the patterns of communication we adopt. All communication generates thoughts and feelings in others. In this section we will look at two ways of encouraging the responses we desire. These are:

1. Questioning our own understanding about people at work.
2. Understanding the different patterns of communication we can adopt and the effect they have.

Motivating the team

chapter 7

Understanding your sales team

We have mentioned the importance of understanding your sales people. In order to do this effectively you might want to look at a number of areas where they need to show improvement.

These might include:

- Willingness to take responsibility
- Showing initiative
- Being committed
- Having a positive attitude
- Being 'solution' based in their approach
- Being customer focused
- Getting on well with colleagues.

A sales manager will need to be realistic about someone's true attitude and level of motivation. To do this you might want to look at your own beliefs and behaviour towards the team. This can affect the way they respond. For example:

- Have positive expectations of people
- Try to be consistent
- Ensure that your intentions are properly understood
- Remain flexible/adaptable.

Monitoring your own behaviour can also help you understand why you react the way you do to certain situations. This will help you manage them better in the future.

Communication patterns

Your level of motivation will be affected by your attitude. Your attitude is a reflection of what you are thinking and feeling at any given moment. What you are focused on and how you feel, will produce a pattern of communication. This, in turn, will influence *how you say something*. Your attitude and tone of communication can be a strong motivational factor in someone deciding whether to listen to what you say.

By taking the time to consider:

- What a person will think
- How they might feel (in response to your communication)
- What you say and how it is interpreted by someone.

You will:

- Think more carefully about what you say
- Improve your chances of being properly understood.

You can do this by understanding the five common patterns that people adopt when communicating:

Pattern 1	Being spontaneous, imaginative and lighthearted.
Pattern 2	Showing concern and understanding.
Pattern 3	Being rational, logical and calm. Inquiring about/seeking information.
Pattern 4	Being resistant, calculating, or tactical.
Pattern 5	Using forceful opinions and judgements.

All of these patterns have their place in communicating with people. While we can be flexible in the patterns we adopt, we will often use one of these patterns more than another. This can tend to be a 'learned' pattern of communication that is more impulsive than controlled. This will depend on the type of person we are and the situation we face.

The challenge is to be able to assess a situation and adopt an appropriate pattern.

Motivating the team

chapter 7

This can be applied to the sales people you manage. You can monitor which pattern they use when communicating with people (externally) and colleagues (internally). You can then work on two fronts:

1. Remain flexible so that you can find appropriate responses to situations and alter a pattern that is not working.

2. Coach your sales people to raise their awareness of the patterns they adopt in selling situations.

You can then use different patterns to communicate with and influence people in different ways.

Flexible communication

Different levels of motivation determine which of these patterns we adopt in our communication. This will be different for each individual. It will also depend on the situation.

As a manager of sales people, you should consider your preferred patterns and consider the effect of your communication on others. Your ability to be flexible in your patterns will determine the impact you have on others and how they respond to you.

A common example of different patterns we adopt can be seen, for example, when a manager approaches a sales person regarding a poor monthly performance:

Sales manager's communication	Sales person's response
The sales manager points out the poor results and states that the sales person must address the situation – now! **(Pattern 5)**	The sales person becomes defensive, referring to lack of support and shows little sign of responding positively to this approach. **(Pattern 4)**

The sales person's 'resistant' response (pattern 4) indicates they do not value or appreciate this communication. The sales manager now has a choice – to stay in pattern 5 or to alter his/her approach to another pattern. Examples of other patterns the manager might now adopt are given below:

Pattern 1	The manager refers to the results in an amusing and friendly manner. The sales person is reminded of their excellent recent results, which may have led them to become over confident this month.
Pattern 2	The manager refers to current results in a concerned manner. The sales person is encouraged to discuss any problems.
Pattern 3	The manager refers to the result in a matter-of-fact tone and asks for the sales person's view and explanation of the current situation. Further questions are asked to determine whether the sales person is taking the necessary steps to reverse the position.
Pattern 4	The manager points out that inconsistency will not earn the sales person a high sales ranking and that their rivals in the team will lead by year-end.

Your goal is not necessarily to match someone else's pattern, but rather to select an appropriate pattern in response.

The diagram opposite develops the above example. The sales manager has communicated forcefully (pattern 5) and receives a resistant response (pattern 4). The manager now decides to take a more flexible line, selecting pattern 2. The sales person responds in pattern 3, allowing a more rational discussion to take place.

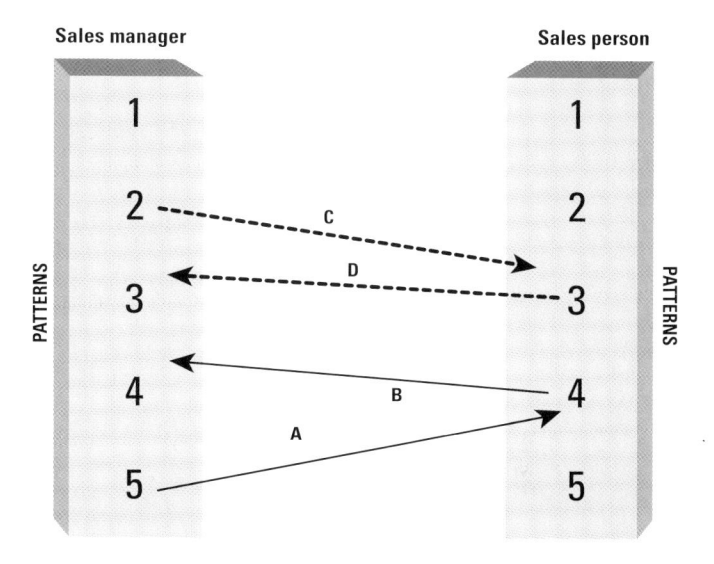

Figure 18: Sales patterns

Your communication to someone (in one pattern) will lead to a reaction in one of the five same patterns. No pattern or approach is necessarily wrong. How appropriate your communication is, will depend on:

- The circumstances
- The response you get.

Pattern 3 represents a rational approach to communication. Therefore, we can use it to be more objective about our delivery of the other patterns. You cannot guarantee the outcome of any communication with someone, however your effectiveness will rely on:

- Focusing on the outcome you want
- Recognising when you receive a poor reaction (a sign that you may need to change your current communication pattern or challenge someone else's).

When we communicate, our body language, tone of voice and words combine to represent our current pattern. How we use these three elements, will influence the patterns and responses we receive from others.

Remember, each pattern can be spoken and received in a positive or negative way. This applies to:

- The content
- The delivery.

The way we communicate will be dependent upon a number of factors:

- The context/urgency of the situation
- Our mood (attitude) and that of the person/people we are talking to
- The subject being discussed
- A person's desired outcome
- The relationship of the people involved.

When you are considering your own pattern of communication with people, consider what outcome you desire. This can provoke choices in our communication we may not have considered. (A lighthearted remark can make someone feel more relaxed in one context and receive a very negative reaction in another.)

A sales manager should therefore be aware of the different types of people he/she manages. You may want to consider what you believe their individual communication patterns to be. By doing this you will improve your own communication skills. You can also encourage your sales people to do the same.

Our beliefs about people's motivation can influence the way we behave with them. We also adopt different patterns of communication with different people. This is dependent on the context of the situation. A flexible approach to this will help to create a positive work environment. It will also help us to understand sales people's behaviour and current level of motivation.

Motivation and reward

Another part of motivating people is to determine what will provide them with a high level of job satisfaction. Sales people respond positively to:

- High earnings
- Recognition/personal achievement
- Opportunities to develop in their role.

A sales manager may have limited control over the financial aspect of the role. However, by being aware of these three aspects you can attempt to:

- Understand someone's personal motivation
- Find flexible alternatives.

There is much you can do to offer opportunities for personal achievement and development. By being aware of what sales people are motivated by, you will be better placed to fulfil them.

Financial reward

A sales person needs to be highly motivated to achieve a company's sales targets. The prospect of exceeding their target should make them feel very positive. However, this will depend on whether they believe they are receiving adequate reward for their effort and that their targets are clearly achievable. Sales targets are discussed in more detail in Chapter 2 – Sales planning – Sales targets.

Motivating the team

The S.M.A.R.T. acronym below provides a sales manager with a method of setting targets in a manner which will raise each person's commitment. Are they:

S = Specific

Targets need to be clearly defined and easy to understand.

M = Measurable

A formula for commission and bonuses needs to be easily measured. Individual results should be available to create a competitive element within the sales team.

A = Agreed

Agreement should be reached with sales people on their individual target. This will help each person 'accept ownership' of the sales target.

R = Realistic

Targets, commission and bonus levels should be achievable and realistic. The reward given is then a strong motivational factor for correct focus and effort.

T = Timed

Create specific time periods for targets to be met. These should be communicated and adhered to.

Incentives

Incentives are an excellent way to focus a sales person's effort. They should be seen as an additional alternative to a sales person's financial remuneration. They are not a substitute for a good commission/bonus structure.

They are a means of creating a specific focus on products and services to increase sales revenue. The time period can extend from short monthly activity periods to an annual one. The type of incentive will depend on the investment you/the company decides to make. It will also depend on:

- The extra revenue you anticipate (during the campaign)
- The reasons for the incentive
- The amount you have budgeted for

Motivating the team

- The product/service you are promoting
- The amount of time you want sales people to focus on it.

Incentives are a good way to focus attention providing they are fair, monitored correctly and achieve the result that was intended.

Non-monetary rewards

Most sales people are driven by opportunities to maximise their income. But they also respond positively to other forms of recognition. This can come in many forms:

- Acknowledgement from you and your senior management
- Special award ceremonies during conferences
- Using particular titles or accolades (such as 'winners' and 'trophies').

Other alternatives are to give different titles to those with particular sales responsibilities. You can also do this with people who have:

- Achieved a high level of results
- Consistently exceeded their level of performance
- The potential to become future sales managers.

A sales person's behaviour will often become more positive and focused when they are given a role with more responsibility. People respond well when they feel appreciated and when they see a way of developing themselves.

In one organisation, the desire to move from 'inside sales' (internal telephone support) to 'outside sales' (face to face selling) provides a steady stream of potential candidates.

A sales manager can maintain a high level of motivation in the sales and support team by being aware of these factors and monitoring people's level of desire.

Education, training and personal development

The provision of training courses reflects the value you place on your team or an individual. **Good training should be seen as an investment not a cost.** By investing in your people and providing opportunities for their development you are demonstrating their value to your company.

To achieve this you will need to determine what their specific needs are. You will also need to identify what relevant programmes are available. By taking the time to do this, you can increase the level of motivation in your sales people. Not only will you improve their skills but you will give someone more chance of improving the quality of their work.

A manager can also select different educational opportunities that will help team members have a better understanding of their role. This will also contribute to a good team atmosphere.

Many people learn more about the importance of trust and co-operation from an 'outward bound' exercise than they might do in the 'classroom'. Regular team meetings and 'corporate entertainment' days can help team members 'bond' with each other. It can also boost each sales person's morale.

Time invested in preparing different methods of reward can produce high motivation and greater commitment from your sales team. Consider combining financial and other types of reward. In this way you will be maintaining focus on the sales target while meeting a person's personal goals and development needs.

Chapter summary

In this chapter we have looked at 'Motivating the team'. This included:

- An individual's goals
- Motivation theory and practice
- Influencing behaviour and attitudes
- Motivation and reward.

A sales manager's goal is to create an environment in which people motivate themselves. This will depend on the way you communicate with the sales team and whether your sales people are satisfied with their job role.

Sales people need to feel that they are understood and appreciated. This forms the basis of them maintaining a high level of motivation.

Checklist

✓ Ensure that company, team and an individual's goals are compatible.

✓ Try and understand what really motivates your sales people.

✓ Monitor the way you/your team communicate with people.

✓ Encourage different incentives to help motivate your sales team.

chapter 8

Personal effectiveness

Introduction

Planning and prioritising

Effective daily routines

Improving your time management skills

Improving your overall effectiveness

Chapter summary

Checklist

Personal effectiveness

Introduction

Sales managers can help to create a motivational environment by demonstrating a structured method of working. One way this can be achieved is by improving their personal effectiveness. This is about the ability to consistently act on the most important sales issues. These include:

- Having a method of staying in control and setting your own agenda
- Being realistic about what you can achieve in a given time
- Managing the quality of contact with people.

The following sections provide guidance that should help you plan and control these aspects of the sales manager's role. You may also find that your sales team can benefit from this too.

Planning and prioritising

In a busy working environment, a sales manager needs to remain focused on the task of helping the team meet their targets. This is done by:

1. Creating plans with timeframes
2. Prioritising
3. Taking time to review.

The first step is to put your plan into manageable timeframes.

Manageable timeframes

Your sales plan will reflect the sales team's goals. How you achieve these requires detailed planning. You will want to identify relevant tasks, projects, and initiatives that you wish to implement. These will need to be broken down into realistic timeframes and put into your weekly/monthly timetable (see Chapter 2 – Sales planning – A sales manager's plan). This will enable you to plan the days and weeks ahead more effectively.

Key aspects of your plan must be to develop:

1. Specific goals for the next year
2. Objectives that will allow you to achieve these goals.

This should include planned actions for a one, three and six month cycle.

Every week, review what you have achieved with your monthly and quarterly objectives. Adjust your plan for the following week. Each day, new items and issues will come onto your agenda. You will be in a better position to assess their priority in relation to your plan if you are constantly monitoring them.

Setting priorities

You should also develop a method of working that will allow you to be flexible and adjust your timetable. You can often lose your perspective and forget to prioritise when you are coping with everyday situations. Constant interruptions and demands on your time may cause this to happen. Unexpected problems can arise, so you will need to assess which items deserve your attention.

One way to help you manage this is to develop a method of prioritising actions (illustrated overleaf). We have called this a **priority circle**. It prioritises actions by importance not just urgency. It will also help you to use your time effectively when there are time pressures.

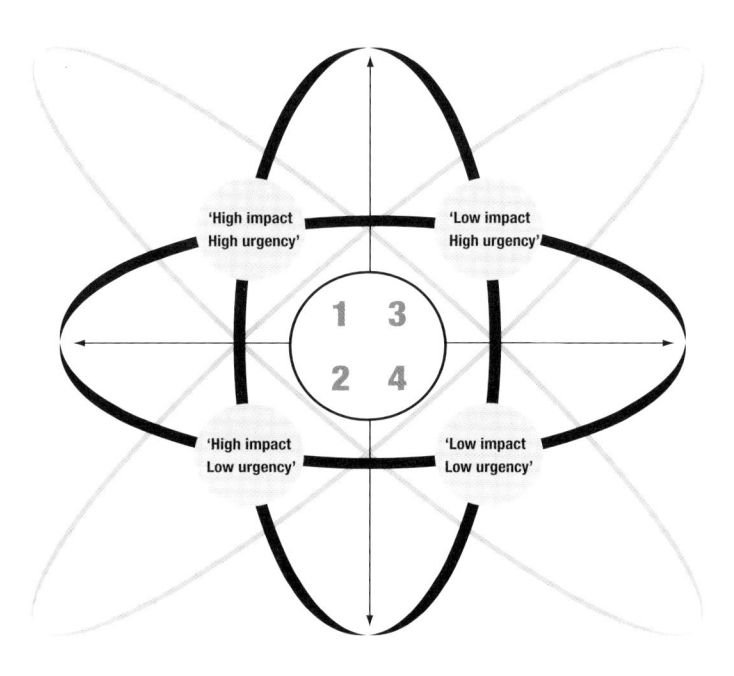

Figure 19: The priority circle

'High impact' tasks

In some companies everything can seem urgent and important. If your company is like this, you will need to assess which items will directly impact on your goals. These need to be put into your timetable and be given a higher priority.

1. Prioritise on the 'High impact' – 'High urgency' items:
   - Decide which are the most important
   - Break these tasks down into definable actions
   - Think of whether any can be delegated (and monitor this)
   - Have deadlines set for each task.

2. Plan the 'High impact' – 'Low urgency' items

   They may not require immediate attention but you must plan how to deal with them. Once again, copy the above steps. 'High impact' tasks with longer deadlines need putting into a schedule. By having the discipline to do this, you avoid everything becoming an urgent priority. It will also help you to decide in what order actions should be done.

'High urgency' tasks

Beware of confusing urgency for importance. 'High urgency' on its own, means that there is a need or request to do something. You can be driven by other people's urgent requirements. If everything is treated as urgent and important you can lose focus and control of your time. This will limit your personal effectiveness.

Many requests on your time can require an immediate response. In order for you to stay in control, consider whether the action is:

- A top priority
- Something that can wait or be resolved later
- Something you should deal with now (so that it does not become a top priority).

This will help you determine whether the item is of high or low impact.

If you monitor this process, you will be able to maximise on the time available. A sales manager must be able to mentally assess priorities on a daily basis. This is difficult when the potential for distraction may be high. In order to overcome these distractions you may want to make decisions about all tasks and communications that you carry out.

While not everything has to be written down, you can use the above four categories (in the circle) to prioritise anything. This might include:

- 'To do' tasks
- Interruptions
- Correspondence (both internal and external)
- Telephone messages
- Electronic mail.

By being aware of the type of interruptions you may get you can be better prepared to deal with them. This will make you more effective and you will feel more in control of events as they occur.

Balance your priorities

Your goals and plans should be communicated to your line manager and your sales team. These should include looking at the priorities as they relate to:

- **Company strategy and objectives**
- **Your sales/business plan objectives.**

Your personal goals should form a part of all this. Tasks that are a low priority will still require completing at a later date. Certain tasks (for example, in the areas of administration) may not seem urgent or very important, but they will need to be done and completing them will help you to be more effective.

How well you translate business objectives into a prioritised set of actions will determine your level of success. Sales managers can face many demands on their time and find it difficult to keep control of their timetable. In order to overcome this, it is vital that they take the time to assess what is important. This type of discipline can be 'passed down' to sales people so that they too focus on how to manage their time well.

Flexibility will also play a key part in this. Your priorities will change and these must be constantly reviewed so that they are reflected in your daily routine and your communication with others.

Effective daily routines

Making the best use of time in a sales manager's professional life can be helped by being well organised on a daily basis. In this section we will look at a number of ideas that you can easily incorporate into your own routine.

Accepting responsibility

A part of a sales manager's daily routine is to know how much to delegate. You have to make conscious decisions on:

- What is your responsibility?
- What is someone else's responsibility?

This is especially important if you find that you are being asked to resolve issues that other colleagues either:

- Do not want to do themselves
- Are unsure of how to deal with.

In order to resolve these issues you will need to:

1. Clarify/discuss the issue with the person (and offer help)
2. Give the issue back to that person (if it is their area of responsibility)
3. Accept that your involvement is/isn't needed (in order to progress/solve the issue).

By taking the time to do this, you will lessen the number of tasks placed upon you that should be dealt with by someone else. Your aim is to avoid people neglecting areas of their responsibility. Encourage your sales people to think about how to solve an issue before they come to you with it. This will help them to be more pro-active and positive.

Personal effectiveness

Managing priorities

Another aspect of ensuring that your daily routines are effective is to create a system to manage your priorities. This will enable you to assess and track important and urgent items. The following approach has two elements to it:

1. A 'To Do' list of actions that are graded in terms of both urgency and importance.
2. A 'Planner' that can help you schedule tasks (on a daily, weekly and monthly basis).

The example below illustrates this with possible tasks a sales manager might have to address in a particular day or week.

1. The daily 'To Do' list

Task	Priority code	Time estimate
Resolve complaint – major account customer	1. 'High urgency – High impact'	1 hour
Plan coaching sessions – 3rd quarter	2. 'Low Urgency – High impact'	1½ hours
Respond to memo from accounts department	3. 'High Urgency Low impact'	½ hour
Prepare monthly sales meeting	2. 'Low urgency – High impact'	½ hour

There are three elements to maintaining the list:

1. Write a short note describing the task.
2. Assign a priority to it (here we have used the priority circle method).

    If two items have the same priority code, you will need to decide which one is the more urgent. Generally, a customer or sales task should be done first. In this case, both items are directly related to the sales team so you may decide to do the task that takes the least amount of time.

3. Assess how long the task will take without interruptions.

Personal effectiveness

chapter 8

The 'To Do' list comprises everything you might possibly do in the period of time you are working. From this you can separate out important items and put them into a planner or diary.

When you do this, consider focusing on the time each action/visit will take. This will allow you to accurately predict the amount of work you are able to do during a day.

2. The Daily/Weekly/Monthly Planner

Weekday	Task	Time estimate
Monday	am Visit major account X	2 hours
	pm Prepare presentation A	1 hour
Tuesday	am Meeting with line manager	1 hour
	Plan sales team meeting	1½ hours
	pm Attend marketing meeting	1½ hours
Wednesday	am Joint visit – sales person Y	2 hours
	pm Review quarterly plan	1½ hours
Thursday	am Sales team meeting	1 hour
	pm Finish presentation A	1½ hours
	Recruitment interview	1½ hours

You will need to take deadlines into account and remember to break down larger tasks into definable actions. These can then be planned into the weeks and months ahead.

An accurate assessment of how long actions take is a key element in managing your time effectively.

In order to maximise your time (and that of your sales people) compare the time you think you will take to complete tasks to how long they actually take. This will give you an understanding of the gap between planned activity and the reality of how long it takes.

You can then help each person (as well as yourself), become better managers of the time available. This will also help everyone in the sales team prioritise better. In order to learn how to do this, you will need to discipline yourself on the length of time it takes to complete daily tasks.

Time estimates

One common challenge in all sales roles is that we can often give ourselves too much to do and too little time to complete it. What we set out to achieve in a day can be unrealistic and does not account for what actually happens. This can be frustrating and lead to a build up of work.

There are three techniques that you can introduce to help control your daily planning:

1. Increase your time estimates by a third

Time can easily be lost when we are not conscious of how long something takes to do or when you experience interruptions. We tend to under-estimate the length of time tasks can take. By increasing the time allowed for each one you allow for unexpected delays. You cannot be totally accurate but it will help you maintain the correct focus.

If you do need more time to complete a task, you can then adjust your present timetable.

2. The Pareto Principle

Vilfredo Pareto, a nineteenth century Italian economist noted that 80% of the wealth in Italy was held by 20% of the population. Companies are often faced with approximately 80% of their business coming from 20% of their customers. This has also come to be known as the 80/20 rule.

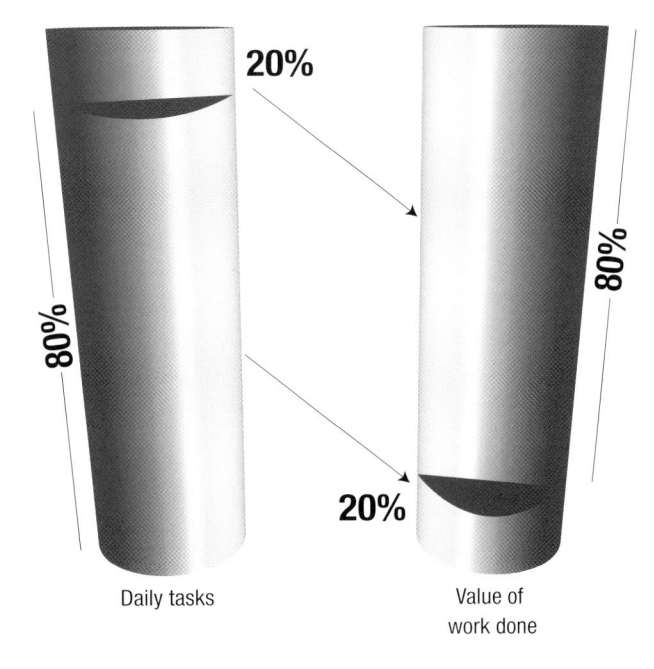

Figure 20: The Pareto Principle

It is this same principle that you can use to get an even better focus on your day. Approximately twenty percent of the tasks you perform will often represent eighty percent of the value of the work you complete.

You may want to look at the daily tasks that you want to achieve and decide which twenty percent are the most important to achieve. If you have ten tasks, select two or three that you particularly want to complete by the end of the day. This will allow you to manage and cope with any interruptions to your schedule.

3. The 50/50 approach to planning

This planning technique assumes that every day, half of your working hours will be taken up with events and tasks you could not anticipate. If you work eight hours a day, on average, then the 50/50 approach suggests that four hours will be taken up by interruptions and unplanned items/actions.

Some of these actions will be High impact – High urgency. Therefore, what you plan to get done in a day, will not always be what you actually do! Generally, you should prepare yourself for the possibility of achieving only four hours worth of work per day that you planned to do. This fits in well with the concept of using time estimates.

Additionally, you can combine this with the Pareto Principle – making sure that the few tasks you plan to do in a day do not represent more than half of your likely working hours. If a task is likely to take more than half a day to complete, you may decide to split the actions up into two-hour tasks in order to achieve this. Although this will make the overall time of completing the task longer, it will allow you to complete other tasks.

If you have a system to manage your tasks, you will be better prepared to re-organise your timetable if your plans need to change.

The benefits of planning this way are that you will:

1. Develop a flexible schedule
2. Agree more realistic deadlines
3. Achieve what you planned to do more consistently.

The average person can only keep seven things in their short-term memory that they can easily recall. As more tasks build up, levels of stress can increase. In order to help you and your sales team keep perspective and stay in control, try and use lists to help prioritise on actions.

Assessing what is achievable everyday will give you (and your sales team) an improved focus. It will also help you achieve what you wanted to, in the time that you estimated. If you have a system to manage your tasks, you will be better prepared to re-organise your timetable if your plans need to change.

Personal effectiveness

chapter 8

Improving your time management skills

In this section we will look at how a sales manager can improve the quality of the time available by looking at the quality of contact he/she maintains with others. There are a number of techniques to achieve this.

Internal contact

Many people internally will request advice, answers and information from a sales manager. You may not be able to fulfil every request immediately, but you will need to deal with each situation in order to avoid further interruptions.

1. Management requests

When your manager gives you tasks to complete, try to determine the deadline for each and put it into your diary. When you are given urgent tasks, list these separately, in the order you intend to do them. You may want to keep a note of what you have done next to each item. This will mean that you are always able to update your line manager when required.

You can also use the list to review the order of all outstanding tasks and to re-negotiate deadlines as appropriate. In this way, you will be proactively managing the relationship.

2. Team requests

Where you are being asked to solve problems or queries, consider developing a policy with your sales team to manage this. This might require the following preparation from them before they approach you:

- Have they spent time thinking about the issue?
- Are they able to explain it quickly and simply?
- Have they come up with a number of alternatives to resolve it?
- Can they recommend one of these as the best solution?

143

Personal effectiveness

This will help you to manage your workload better and encourage your sales people to think for themselves. In the same way, you can adopt this approach when communicating with your own line manager.

3. Prioritising tasks

Managing your time with the sales team and colleagues is an important part of any managerial role. How you do this will influence people's perception of you effectiveness. With constant time pressures this can often be difficult to control.

'High impact – High urgency' items should be dealt with as soon as possible. For other lower priority items, keep a list of the people you need to call. You can act on these at convenient moments during the day and week.

By managing your time well, you provide an example to your team. As you work through these lists, focus on one category at a time – telephone calls electronic mail etc.

Improving your overall effectiveness

Even though we prioritise our time and commit ourselves to a plan there can still be reasons why we do not get the results we seek. These 'blocks' are not always easy to identify or resolve. Some will relate to ineffective personal routines – habits and practices that we are unaware of. Others will relate to external factors. These might include how we manage relationships at work.

Identifying the blocks

A sales manager should try and reduce the effect of these 'blocks' or try and dispose of them. The following table will help you identify them and assess their effect. You can then prioritise on any action you decide to take. It is worth repeating this exercise occasionally so that you measure your level of success in dealing with them.

There are ten reasons listed opposite why a sales manager can lose control of their time. You may want to select which of these are your top three, biggest 'time-eaters'. Then look at how you can try and manage these better in order to improve your efficiency and maximise on the time available.

The top ten 'time-eaters' *Rank order*

▶ Unclear of your objectives/priorities ☐

▶ Constant changing of priorities ☐

▶ Attempting to do too much ☐

▶ Personal organisation ☐

▶ Interruptions ☐

▶ Inability to say 'no'/let someone down ☐

▶ Self-discipline ☐

▶ Delegation ☐

▶ Too many meetings/appointments ☐

▶ Delaying decisions ☐

By taking the time to do this you will identify aspects of your communication and time management that can be improved.

Personal and external 'time-eaters'

The next step is to identify which items are:

- Personal characteristics (that you have some control over)
- External (which you may have little/no control over).

Personal

You may want to address the personal issues first. Try to identify the relevant actions or tasks that will create the improvement you seek. If you implement these regularly they will become a habit.

If you can improve your own business behaviour you will improve your managerial effectiveness and set a good example to your sales team. This may well have a positive impact on team morale and discipline.

External 'time-eaters'

There are times when a sales manager might be called into an unexpected meeting. This can mean that although you plan your day (and therefore your week), you will have to remain flexible.

However, external 'time-eaters' occur in any management role. Again, use this as an opportunity to assess how you might control or lessen the impact of regular time-eaters. If you can retain a calm, professional manner, you will be able to concentrate on deciding the best course of action.

At times, you will need to influence someone else's behaviour by helping that person plan their time. Your aim is to control your own agenda. The more you can do this, the more effective you will be.

Taking your time

The nature of a sales manager's role means that you will be under constant time pressures. This can mean that you do not:

- Take the time to consider how to deal with something
- Challenge information (to ensure that you understand/agree it).

Therefore, an important element of communication is to remember that it is a two-way process. Allow time to give someone else an opportunity to assess information from you. You might also want to request time to do the same when receiving information or a task. By having respect for your own time, you will encourage other people to do the same.

Having a break

It has been shown that a person's level of concentration diminishes after fifty minutes without having a break. Therefore, by having an occasional break, you will increase your level of effectiveness. This can be difficult in a sales environment but if you can slow down the pace of your work it will improve the quality of it, and help you to remain relaxed.

Sales managers need to filter and control the tasks they plan on a daily basis. Their ability to manage contact with others will be a measure of their effectiveness. This is best achieved through reviewing a plan after it has been put into action.

Chapter summary

In this chapter we have looked at 'Personal effectiveness'. This included:

- Planning and prioritising
- Effective daily routines
- Improving your time management skills.

Personal effectiveness requires good organisation and planning. It means making the most of your sales team's time and their resources. Give yourself time to analyse and reflect on work situations as this will help you make better decisions. Time is a limited resource, so we need to respect this. The correct use of it will also help you become a better manager and an example to your team.

Personal effectiveness

chapter 8

Checklist

- ✓ Have clear priorities and work to manageable timeframes.
- ✓ Keep lists of tasks and review your progress.
- ✓ Manage and control your interaction with others.
- ✓ Try to identify what will make you more effective (and commit to acting upon it).

chapter 9

Managing change

Introduction

Factors affecting change

Analysing a need for change

Resistance to change

Involving people in the change process

Chapter summary

Checklist

Introduction

A sales manager has some control over how he/she manages their time but far less over the degree of change that can take place in their own company. Often, uncertainty and the speed of change can bring real challenges to a sales environment.

We will now discuss:

- How sales people react to a changing situation
- Why companies want to change
- Why people can be fearful of trying to do something new or different
- The best ways of gaining commitment to the change process.

Not everyone interprets change in the same way. However, by adapting to change, sales managers are better preparing their sales people for the future.

Factors affecting change

It is natural for people to feel uncomfortable if they believe their job role will become more difficult after new measures are brought in. As today's companies try to find ways to sell more of their products and services, changes will occur frequently. This might apply to factors affecting your company, or your industry. It could be due to government legislation, a company merger or site closure.

Change is, therefore, about adjusting to a set of new and different circumstances. It could be within your control or outside of it. It might be with your approval or without it.

People understand and react to change differently. Your sales team will get used to a certain way of working and grow to feel comfortable in that environment. In the next section we will look at the type of changes that can occur and what control we may have over them.

Managing change

chapter 9

Internal and external factors

Change in a sales environment can be internally or externally driven. How the sales manager proposes to manage this will depend on what is being introduced. Some of the most common factors affecting change can be shown in the following way.

Internal factors affecting change	External factors affecting change
New sales personnel	Demand for your product/service
New products coming out	Change in the number of suppliers in your industry
Change in company structure	Suppliers to your company
Change in work procedures	Company take over
New sales targets	A recession or economic boom
Change of Directors in the company	New technology
Your relationship with your colleagues	Your own domestic situation

Some factors affecting change in an organisation will be out of your control. However, part of the sales manager's role is to anticipate change and to prepare for the task of managing its impact on the sales operation.

Adapting to this both internally and externally is also about education. You can help by finding ways of sharing information with the team about current trends. This can be done in various ways:

- A presentation at a team meeting
- Distributing copies of a relevant newspaper article
- Showing selected video/Compact Disc (CD) material
- Inviting a guest speaker to address the sales team.

Introducing change internally

Introducing change internally can come from the desire to:

1. Increase sales/productivity.
2. Improve the quality of your product or service, staff motivation and the relationship with existing customers, prospects and suspects.
3. Reduce costs.

These initiatives may be driven by different levels of management in a company, depending on where the desire to change originated and why it is being sought. **Whatever the reason for change and whoever is driving it, there is normally a pressure to consistently over achieve!**

This is the nature of selling and it can bring with it, a degree of stress. If this is well managed, then sales people will remain committed to the company. If it is not, it can create a loss of confidence and some of the team may even decide to leave.

A strong motivation to change something is often related to a company's growth ambitions/market share and how to increase it. Senior management may alter their strategy if they find it is not working. If an initiative is handled properly a team of sales people should remain motivated.

There are a number of other factors that determine the success of any change process. These will be based on:

1. How effectively it is introduced
2. Whether the sales team have been properly involved in the process
3. What feedback the sales team receive throughout the process
4. Whether they receive incentives and rewards for meeting new targets and implementing the changes properly.

All these factors demand a high degree of communication skills. The sales manager's task is to remove as much uncertainty as possible and to show clear leadership and direction.

Politics

The culture of your company is also a significant factor in managing change. A sales manager will need to assess how this is viewed by his/her team. Their reaction can be understood by studying:

- The history of your company
- The industry you are in and your traditional markets
- The current influence of different departments and managers
- The average length of time sales people have been in their job
- Whether change is a common occurrence.

Every company has its own culture and way of managing it's staff. It is important for every sales manager to be aware of this. You should also make the sales team aware of the positive elements of any proposed change.

By understanding the type of company you are working for, managing change becomes easier. No company is exactly the same, even if they sell the same type of product or service. A sales manager can learn from the internal structure and the interaction between different managerial levels and different departments.

Change is now part of a sales manager's everyday life. It can offer opportunities as well as cause uncertainty for the team. There are many factors affecting it. These have to be understood so that you can prepare yourself and the sales team properly.

Analysing a need for change

There has to be a good reason to do something differently and this must be communicated clearly by a sales manager. Constant change that is not understood and appears to offer no benefits can lead to confusion. This may affect each person's sales performance.

Before you change something (whether you are the instigator or not), think about the consequences of it and how it is best managed. Some decisions will be forced upon you. This can mean that you have little or no control over them. But even if this is the case you can still try to manage this effectively.

Assessing the situation

Perhaps the first priority of a sales manager introducing new practices is to assess the current situation correctly. This means understanding the context – comparing the past to the present. It also looks at future possibilities.

The three phases affecting change are:

WHERE WERE YOU?
Illustrates how you adapted and managed past changes

▼

WHERE ARE YOU?
Provides a link to what you did and what you need to do

▼

WHERE DO YOU WANT TO BE?
Helps clarify your future vision and prepare the way ahead

Figure 21: Phases affecting change

Managing change

By considering these three factors you maximise your chances of successfully applying any new business practises.

Understanding the objective

If you are looking to make changes internally there are four main areas to consider that will affect you and your sales team. Any one of these areas might also affect another. The four areas are:

1. The work people do
2. The existing structure of the company
3. The culture of the company you work for
4. The individuals who report to you.

In many ways analysing a new challenge is about preparation and planning. The degree of success you will have could depend on your interpretation and delivery of the proposed change.

By sharing selected information with your sales team (providing this is possible) and getting their approval, you will increase your chances of success. It will be a test of your leadership skills and will require a degree of diplomacy and sensitivity.

A sales manager had to announce at the beginning of a New Year that targets had increased. At the same time, the team was also trying to cope with the introduction of an important new product. The manager decided to ask an experienced (and high performing) sales person to contribute towards the presentation and to focus on the positive aspects of the pay plan.

The emphasis was on the potential for increasing income. Therefore, by discussing the issues with the team, the sales manager found it easier to gain their acceptance. His willingness to involve, listen and respond in this way enabled the changes to be more effective. That year, the district exceeded their new target.

Levels of change

Part of the preparation and planning for any change will involve two factors:

1. The degree of difficulty
2. How long it will take to achieve specified goals.

This will largely be determined by the impact on different managerial levels and departments. It can take time for change to properly filter through to certain parts of a company. The diagram below illustrates the likely relationship between these two factors.

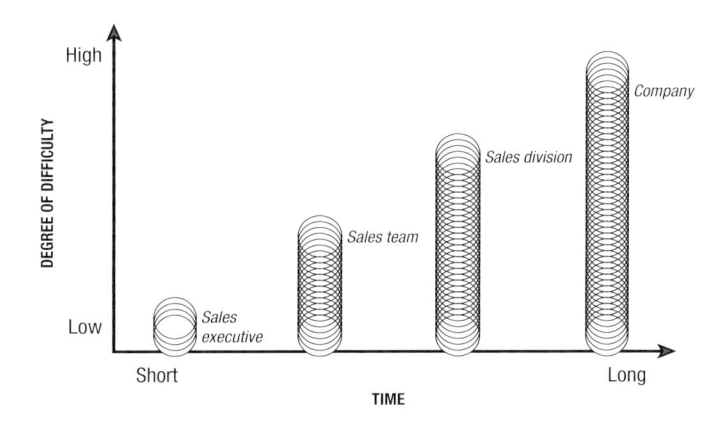

Figure 22: Time factors affecting levels of change

If a company introduces a high degree of change, it will take much longer to implement than something for one individual. A change to one part of a company or division can have an effect on other people in another part.

A sales manager may not have all the necessary information to predict how long it will take for a change to work. But if they are to manage the situation successfully, they will need to find this out and assess the likely impact on their sales people.

If two companies were to merge, the degree of time it would take to bring them together may be measured in months, perhaps years. Introducing a change to an individual's working practice could take only a number of days or weeks.

Managing change

chapter 9

Sales managers increase their chances of achieving their objective if enough thought is given to the level of change required and its effect on people. Another factor to consider is how well something new is implemented. You should ensure that any changes affecting the sales team become part of each person's everyday behaviour. If this is not done, they have less chance of wanting to revert back to previous work routines.

For sales managers, the success of managing a change may depend on three factors:

1. The strength of their relationship with the sales team
2. The relationship they have at different managerial levels
3. How well they communicate with other internal departments.

In order to analyse a need for change it is important to look at the different roles of the people the change is designed for. You should also look at who is most affected by it and how you can make a person feel part of the process. People need managing in different ways and this must be taken into consideration. A correct analysis of the situation will help you manage changes more effectively.

Resistance to change

Many people are actually fearful of change. A new set of circumstances can make us feel uncomfortable and wary.

There are normally three main responses to this. These are to:

1. Embrace it
2. Accept it
3. Resist it.

It is the third aspect that we will now deal with – resistance to change.

Forcing change through

You may be able to influence whether/how something should change. If this happens, you will have a certain amount of control over the outcome. However, many decisions involving change are made at a senior management level and involve a directive being given to the whole company.

This can cause friction and negativity if people see the change as an imposition. They may feel that they have not been consulted or that there is little concern for their job role. If any changes you make are met with resistance, the chances of success will depend on:

- The strength of character of the individuals concerned
- Your determination to see it through.

If the driving force of the change is stronger than the resisting force, it is more likely to be effective.

It is unlikely that a corporate decision will be reversed. A sales manager will, therefore, be faced with the task of trying to achieve the right level of acceptance and commitment from the sales team.

You might face resistance to a company directive and find it difficult to re-focus certain members of the team. Therefore, before taking any action, assess the degree of support within the sales operation and the strength of any opposition. For example, influence may be brought to bear through other people rather than direct action.

The following table is one method of assessing the forces you are dealing with in this area. Change will be interpreted differently. Some people will see the change as offering them positive opportunities – they are the 'winners'. Others will see themselves as the 'losers'.

Relative power and influence

	LOW	HIGH
WINNERS	1. Tele-sales team *New income opportunities*	2. Senior account managers *See opportunity to increase income on other products*
LOSERS	3. Support team *Will have more sales support work to do*	4. Junior account managers *Commission affected*

Figure 23: Winners and losers of change

By looking at change in this way, a sales manager is able to assess the impact of a new initiative. The telesales team (1) will now be able to sell a number of products previously sold by account managers. They see this as an advantage.

The senior account managers (2), have perceived greater income opportunities and will also support the change. The task will be to convince the support team (3) and junior account managers (4).

If you can determine why people see themselves as losers or winners you can then develop a plan to help them. For example, you may wish to get support from experienced members of the sales and support teams. With their co-operation the initiative will be more likely to succeed.

The strength of someone's resistance will affect how you manage that person. Many people will have no clear opinion and may not see new work practices as a win or lose situation. These might include junior or new sales people who have no previous experience in the company. Their expectations could be lower because of this and you should find that they accept changes more easily.

Reasons for resistance

In order to manage change better, a sales manager needs to understand the reasons why someone is resisting. People resist for many reasons. These include:

- **They do not believe they will benefit**

Sales people are trained to assess a situation independently. This can cause a degree of resistance if their perception of a situation differs from the management view. Suspicion and misunderstanding can set in when a sales person believes they will be worse off after a change has taken place.

- **They do not understand the change**

Sometimes company directive will not be communicated very well. If this is the case, sales people may not have fully understood it. They may not want to confront their fear of change and therefore choose to resist it.

- **They do not like the change**

If someone dislikes the change, it gives that person a reason to resist it – or ignore it!

- **Resentment**

Some might feel that the change has been forced upon them. People rarely like something that is imposed on them without consultation or agreement. Alienation arises from lack of involvement in the decision-making process. This can lead to disruption.

- **They are tired of constant changes**

Many companies are constantly altering day-to-day working procedures. This can cause frustration and a hardening of attitudes toward new initiatives. This can cause a reluctance to appreciate the benefits of a change.

- **They may have had a previous bad experience**

A bad experience resulting from a previous company directive may cause resistance to it. Someone may have disagreed with a previous change and witnessed a negative outcome. This will affect their attitude when interpreting the effect of future initiatives.

- **Fear that a change may expose them**

Many people resist change because they fear new skills will be introduced which will expose them. They fear that they may not be able to adapt to meet the new company expectations.

All of these reasons require opportunities for discussion and a sensitive response. This can be discussed individually or with the team. The degree of resistance will be determined by:

- The strength of someone's personality
- The number of people involved (in resisting) their attitude
- The influence of individual team members.

If a sales manager can see that a majority of the team support the change, he/she can use this to influence those who still resist it.

With the number of changes sales people are expected to make every year, many may be wary of new measures. You need to manage the change process carefully and you should not be surprised to meet some resistance.

A skilled manager will analyse a situation before they attempt to implement a change. We can now look at ways in which to prepare for this.

Involving people in the change process

In order to introduce changes successfully, try and involve your line manager and your sales team in the process. This should make people feel part of it. You might not be able to control the change itself. However, you can use this to your advantage, as you are in the same position as your staff.

A sales manager needs to be sympathetic yet firm. Involvement shows respect and concern. It will help you receive the support of your team. They will find it easier to understand if they feel that you are considering their interests as well as your own.

Ways to gain commitment

The main ways to gain people's support in the change process include:

1. Communication

By talking to people as a group and on an individual level you will find out about any fears they might have. With this information you can gauge the reaction to a change and assess how it will affect your team's sales performance.

2. Education

People often feel threatened by change if it means that they have to learn new skills. You may need to find out if training measures are going to be introduced or education provided. This can lessen the resistance and reassure people that they will cope in the future.

3. Group discussion

Whatever measures are being introduced, they will still have to be implemented properly. Discussion with those who will be most affected can lead to them giving their approval.

4. Support

People who worry about change may have concerns that can be overcome if they know that they have your support. Some people are too proud to ask for help at a time when they most need it. It can also be reassuring to know that your sales manager will support you during this time.

5. Negotiation

For those people who are strong willed and who resist new measures, a degree of negotiation may be needed to gain their support. By reaching an agreement you increase the chances of the change being effective. You also reduce the chances of someone becoming uncooperative and a potentially destructive force.

A degree of manipulation might be necessary. It could involve altering a person's role or offering them some incentive to influence them. You may be able to use persuasion as a way of trying to bring people round to your point of view.

Managing change

6. Dominance

This should be a sales manager's last resort. It requires a more forceful approach and could be a test of the respect and loyalty the team has for their manager. There are two key elements to this approach:

- Describe their behaviour, its effect, your feelings and your future expectation (See Chapter 6 – Communication and development – Appraisal.)
- To explain the reasons and benefits for the change and to reinforce the fact that it will go ahead with or without their co-operation.

This approach has advantages because it prompts an instant response and you have the opportunity of dealing with issues immediately. However, it can cause resentment and actually create further resistance. Your leadership skills will be called upon to manage this type of situation effectively.

Ideally this approach will not be necessary and you will be able to try one (or a combination) of the methods we have described.

Steps involved in the change process

No amount of planning and preparation can prepare a sales manager for every changing situation. However, if you are involved in making changes there are a number of steps to consider. These are to:

- **Analyse**
- **Prepare**
- **Involve**
- **Communicate**
- **Implement**
- **Monitor.**

There are times when the steps will not come in this order. For example, you may decide to involve your sales team earlier in the change process.

The key to involving any group of people is to be adaptable. If you can give them the opportunity to contribute, this might be enough to achieve their full co-operation.

Managing change

chapter 9

A sales manager's approach will have a large influence on how any new changes will be perceived. If you see this as an opportunity it will be reflected by many of your staff. It will set the tone for future behaviour and shorten the time taken for people to adjust.

Chapter summary

In this chapter we have looked at 'Managing change'. This included:

- Factors affecting change
- Analysing a need for change
- Resistance to change
- Involving people in the change process.

'Change management' has become a common occurrence in business. The success of any company can depend on what to change, when and how often. Introducing new measures will often put a company in a stronger position to compete in the future. Sales managers need to be flexible, sensitive and adaptable when deciding how to manage change.

Checklist

✓ Many factors affect change both internally and externally.

✓ There are different levels of change (each taking different amounts of time).

✓ People often resist change (and the reasons for this need to be identified).

✓ A change has to be monitored in order to measure its success.

✓ Where possible involve people in the change process.

chapter 10

Recruitment

Introduction

Defining the sales role

Setting parameters

Assessment

Interviewing and induction

Chapter summary

Checklist

Recruitment

chapter 10

Introduction

Recruiting sales people can be a costly investment – if you include training, a company car, salary and bonuses. There are three areas we can focus on to illustrate how important recruiting the right people is. These include:

- Defining the role
- Assessing candidates correctly
- Developing skills to help sales performance.

Finding the right people is not easy, there are a number of things you can do to improve your chances of selecting the right candidates.

Defining the sales role

Defining the sales role correctly will help reduce the need to continually replace and recruit sales people. A manager has to be flexible when it comes to recruiting someone for a sales position. A high turnover of employees can:

- Have a big impact on your recruitment costs
- Lower the morale of those who remain
- Put a greater strain on a sales manager
- Make sales targets harder to achieve
- Make it more difficult for a company to plan effectively.

It is therefore important to create a sales role that is stimulating, rewarding and motivational.

Employing the right people

Sales managers can increase the chances of recruiting people successfully by:

1. **Employing the right person for the role** – accepting someone who has the capability of meeting the job specification.

2. **Employing a person who can fulfil most of the role** – accepting someone who has the potential to fully meet the job specification with the right support.

If you employ someone who can be developed for a sales position, you will need to give them support and encouragement. Sometimes a person may be able to fulfil the role you have created after:

- Proper training
- Some experience in another role
- Spending time with an existing sales person.

Freedom in a role

In order to help someone in a new role:

- Give them some freedom and responsibility
- Make them accountable for their actions
- Share certain information with them (to communicate the company's goals).

By giving sales people a degree of autonomy over their day-to-day working lives, you will help to increase their confidence. This should encourage a degree of loyalty and trust. By considering this you are also thinking about how the person can make the role a success. This will help you to evaluate their progress.

Recruitment

chapter 10

Sales development

Most sales roles have a life span. You should therefore think about how long to keep someone in a position. This will enable you to assess any aspects of the role that are not being carried out properly at an earlier stage. By increasing job satisfaction you may reduce staff turnover.

The more stable your sales force is, the more impact they are likely to have in the marketplace.

If you think that a member of your staff is reaching a point where they need a new challenge, consider changing their role. This will also give new opportunities to other members of the sales team.

You may want to consider carrying out exit interviews whenever a sales person leaves. You will probably receive more honest feedback at this time than at any other. This may also help you to address any issues that may have contributed to that person leaving, for example, a commission/bonus scheme.

A company experienced a twenty-five percent reduction in sales on some of their leading brand items in a matter of months. Many districts in the country were finding it harder to meet the sales target (even though it had not increased dramatically). Many sales managers did not know how to increase demand and price levels.

Analysis revealed that:

- Recruitment and development had not been a priority
- People's selling skills had not been properly developed
- The company focused on price issues (more than quality/service/application)
- Some sales people would not succeed in the current market
- The sales role would need to be reviewed.

These issues were not looked into when market prices were stable. After this analysis the company decided to improve the skills of existing personnel. Creating a sales development programme achieved this.

Recruitment

chapter 10

Setting parameters

An awareness of the requirements for a sales role will contribute to the selection of good candidates. Recruitment and selection can still be a subjective process. Intuition is an important indicator in deciding on whether someone is right for a role (see Chapter 5 – Managing the sale – Analysing sales behaviour). There are also a number of other factors to consider.

Where possible, work with your personnel department to:
- Agree the role they/you will play in the process
- Assess the level of interviewing skill levels
- Set parameters that will govern the decision-making process.

One way of bringing objectivity and a structure to the process is by setting parameters.

1. Ensure you know the difference between what you:
   - **Would like to have**
   - **Must have.**

   This may relate to particular skills, technical knowledge, professional qualifications, level of experience etc. You are providing a useful filter to ensure you progress with the right candidates.

2. Consider the person's attitude as well as their technical ability. A positive attitude in a sales role is essential.

3. Look at the qualities needed for the role. A sales person will need to achieve and exceed a sales target. This will require sales ability, organisation skills, patience and persistence.

4. Ensure that all candidates meet the company's required standard. This might mean considering a review of your method of attracting applicants.

5. Consider involving other people in the interview process. This could be another member of the management team or a senior sales person. A colleague might see something differently from you and this will help you to remain objective.

Recruitment

chapter 10

Every sales person needs to feel that they are being developed in their role. This is applicable regardless of how long they stay with a company. Getting the right people initially can help to reduce staff turnover. Whoever you decide to recruit, all sales people should be:

- Well trained
- Motivated
- Well rewarded.

Looking at the development of sales people takes time. (It may also need to be done with help from your personnel department.) Setting parameters for recruitment enables you to prepare for a balanced approach to selecting the right candidate.

Assessment

To help you select the right people you should list the criteria you require from a candidate. You will also want to take into account the current state of the market against anticipated future developments.

This will involve:

- Looking at market trends (and comparing them to your future expectations)
- The implications that this will have for the sales role you require
- Prioritising and assessing the knowledge, skills and attitude required of a new recruit
- Looking at the internal needs of your own company.

Guidelines for assessment

Here are some guidelines for assessing prospective candidates:

1. CV's

Study a candidate's Curriculum Vitae (CV). Note how long a person stayed in a job role. This is an indication of commitment, reliability loyalty and experience. Look for aspects where more information could be provided. A good example of this is to look at the reasons given for leaving or changing jobs.

2. Previous role

Look at what someone achieved and contributed in previous job roles. This might be more important than a list of their responsibilities. You should also ask for references and be prepared to follow them up.

3. Skill sets needed in the role

Identify the skills sets needed for the job. Decide what type of person you would like to employ. Look at a person's attitude and compare this with how you would like someone to behave.

Further evidence of these can be identified from:

- Previous work experience
- Interaction with past customers
- Achievements at school/college
- Hobbies/interests
- Their attitude to your company/industry/products/service.

4. Interpersonal skills

Sales people should develop a positive relationship with their suspects, prospects and customers. This will require good interpersonal skills. Their choice of words and approach with people needs to be appropriate. Look at their ability to interact with you and others during the interview process.

5. Organisational ability

You will also be looking for someone who is focused, determined and well organised. A sales role will require someone to assess a situation correctly. Good organisational ability will encourage this.

6. Involving the candidate

You may want to ask a candidate's opinion about a challenge they might face in their job role – or one that they faced in the past – 'How did you…?' 'What would you do if …?'. This can reveal something about their level of ability and suitability.

7. Number of interviewers

You may want to use multiple selection methods (or you may be asked to by your personnel department/line manager). An initial screening process could be followed by a dual interview. You could also use different interviewers at each stage. By doing this, an interviewer will often see things that another has missed.

8. Introduce the sales team

You can also consider meeting candidates with your sales team as a group or individually. This would be an informal part of the process, which might uncover aspects of the candidates personality which you had not seen.

9. Profiling

It is now common to use computer-based methods to 'screen' a candidate before interviewing them. There are companies that specialise in helping you by creating questionnaires for candidates to complete. This is called psychometric testing and might focus on areas such as:

- Interpersonal skills
- Leadership
- Business awareness
- Analytical capabilities
- Operational qualities
- Assertiveness
- Business relationships.

In the example below are of some of the areas covered in a profile:

The person	
Interpersonal skills	**Leadership**
Good team 'player'	Can accept responsibility
Honest/confident	Can motivate others
Good communicator	Able to assess situations correctly
Hard worker	Capable of making decisions
Ability to work under pressure	
Good at building business relationships	

Business skills	
Business awareness	**Analytical capabilities**
Organisational skills	Technical ability
Self development	Analysing problems
Aware of developments in the industry	Numeric skills (PC ability)
Commercial experience	Written ability
Competitor awareness	
Product awareness	

Figure 24: Sales profile competency chart

Profiling is a useful way of looking at a candidate's ability to deal with work related issues. It will also give you more information about their character. It should be used as part of the selection process, not as the primary method of selection. This is because you are relying on a candidate's perception of how they see themselves and this may differ from how they might actually perform in the role.

Recruitment

Criteria for selection

In this section we will introduce a method of helping a sales manager measure a person's ability in the following key areas:

- Knowledge
- Attitude
- Skills.

This is further illustrated in the assessment table opposite where we have completed the knowledge section only. In Chapter 6 - Communication and development - Appraisal, we use the same process for appraising performance.

The steps are:

1. Select your criteria for the role and determine a score to reflect the degree of capability you seek for each candidate.

2. Assess whether a candidate is over or under qualified compared to your required level (1= low capability, 5 = average capability, 9 = high capability).

You might also want to prioritise on the importance of a particular section or subject. In the assessment table, selling skills, for example, could be a key factor in your selection process. Remember this will put you in a better position to make a more objective evaluation of a candidate's suitability for the role.

- The square indicates the standard you seek
- The circle, your assessment of the candidate.

Recruitment

chapter 10

Scoring

1 = poor

3 = below standard

5 = average

7 = very good

9 = excellent

SUBJECT	EVALUATION
KNOWLEDGE	
Industry	1 3 5 ⑦ 9
Products	1 3 5 ⑦ 9
IT capability	1 ③ 5 7 9
SKILLS	
Planning/time management	1 3 5 7 9
Hi level negotiation	1 3 5 7 9
Board level presentations	1 3 5 7 9
Developing relationships	1 3 5 7 9
Problem solving	1 3 5 7 9
Interpersonal skills	1 3 5 7 9
ATTITUDES	
Positive and enthusiastic	1 3 5 7 9
Initiative	1 3 5 7 9
Dress code	1 3 5 7 9

Figure 25: Assessment table

The standard required for the knowledge section criteria suggests:

- A high amount of industry knowledge is required
- Less product knowledge is required
- High IT capability is needed.

In our example, the candidate's industry knowledge is close to the required standard, while product knowledge exceeds it. A lack of IT capability is particularly evident.

175

The advantage of this format is that you can evaluate candidates in a more objective way. When faced with a number of strong contenders you will be looking for specific differences in each one. This will separate them and help you to decide their suitability for the role.

Once you determine that certain candidates have the correct profile, you are in a better position to allow other factors (personality, attitude) to influence your decision-making.

Correct assessment of candidates in the selection process requires preparation and planning. By taking the time to do this you are more likely to choose the right person. This will improve the chances of that person staying with the company, fulfilling their potential in their sales role and fitting in with other members of your sales team.

Interviewing and induction

Interviewing is another key part of the selection process. Much of this skill is based on asking the right questions, listening to the answers and observing the right body language. Your ability to relax the candidate may encourage them to give you a more realistic assessment of their character.

Format for the interview

The structure for the interview should cover certain key areas. These include:

1. Provide a welcoming and friendly atmosphere. Consider:
   - Where they have to wait
   - What the interview room is like
   - How they are treated from the moment they arrive.

Remember that the candidate is assessing your company too!

2. Have a number of general, open questions. Some of these might be based on what you have seen in a candidate's CV. This will encourage the person to relax and talk in a more natural manner.

3. Focus on what candidates achieved in previous jobs they held. Assess what they contributed and how they made a difference to the role. While a job specification can look very impressive, you want to look at the calibre of the individual. This can be measured in terms of results they achieved and the context of how this was done.

4. Try and identify what the person enjoyed doing in each job role and what he/she was best at. You might also want to find out what the person liked and disliked. Where someone has no previous experience, make a comparison in the way they approached their studies, sports and interests.

5. Look for items in their CV that stand out. Ask the candidate to explain these. You are not trying to put someone under pressure. You are trying to ensure that you have all the relevant information before making a decision.

6. Discuss their salary (and commission/bonus) expectations and the methods of payment they are used to.

7. Check what preparation the candidate has made to understand your company – whether they have studied your company report, product literature or visited your website.

8. Look at the expectation they have of the job they are applying for. Make them aware of what is involved. Discuss any areas that either of you feel might need special training/coaching.

9. Ask a candidate if there is any information that they would like to know. This can be a useful indicator for you to measure their level of awareness and desire for the new role.

A good interviewing technique is largely based on the ability to:

1. Ask the right questions
2. Listen carefully to the responses
3. Cross reference the answers to your own perception/knowledge
4. Probe for further information
5. Compare information to the candidate's previous statements
6. Assess him/her against a profile/set of criteria.

The more prepared you are, the more you will be able to use these skills effectively during interviews.

Induction

Once you have decided on a candidate, the next step is to introduce them to other relevant people in your company. The highest motivational point for any member of staff will be during the first month of their job. Their expectation will be high and this will be your best opportunity to create the right environment for them to succeed.

An induction programme

When a new member of staff joins your company consider how they can be introduced to other members of staff and what actions are needed to achieve this. An induction programme should include:

1. Commitment from the sales manager to provide support and spend some time with the new sales person.
2. A timetable designed by the manager/personnel department for the weeks ahead. Familiarise new sales people with:
   - The culture, beliefs and values of the company/sales team
   - Product/PC sales training
   - Sales processes and systems

Recruitment

chapter 10

- The function of other departments (and how they relate to sales)
- The heads of different departments (and key personnel)
- The sales team and how it operates.

3. An opportunity for new recruits to ask questions about aspects of their role. This will help them feel reassured and adjust to your company culture.

4. Co-operation from a previous territory sales person/caretaker of an area (where possible). Visits to relevant new business and existing accounts to understand likely issues.

A sales person will perform better when they are given a good introduction to a new company and a good understanding of their new role.

Benefits of a good induction programme

Other benefits of introducing a good induction programme are:

1. The new recruit will produce results quicker.
2. There will be less need for support and coaching.
3. He/she will feel more confident (and this will increase the person's effort and level of commitment).
4. You reduce the chances of high staff turnover.
5. Your sales support departments will spend less time assisting and answering queries.

People can feel unsure of the new position they find themselves in. Therefore, the quicker a person settles into a new sales role, the quicker you can expect results from them. A good induction programme will give someone confidence, which, in turn, will help their sales performance.

By taking the time to prepare for an interview you will save time later in the process. This will increase your chances of getting the right person for the vacant job role.

Recruitment

chapter 10

When sales people join a company they often see this as a new opportunity in their lives. This means that they begin with a positive impression of the organisation, its products/services and people. A well-planned induction programme can capture their enthusiasm and can be used to make a positive impact on the team and the sales target.

Chapter summary

In this chapter we have looked at 'Recruitment'. This included:

- Designing the sales role
- Assessment
- Interviewing and induction

Time spent recruiting good sales people should be seen as an investment. By selecting the right criteria and creating a structured approach to the recruitment process you stand a better chance of achieving this.

Checklist

✓ Specify the knowledge, skills and attributes you require.

✓ When recruiting, match the right person to the right role.

✓ Develop an interview structure and an objective means of assessment.

✓ Support recruitment with a well thought out induction programme.

chapter 11

Selling through indirect channels

Introduction

Challenges and benefits

Managing indirect channels

Chapter summary

Checklist

Selling through indirect channels

chapter 11

Introduction

The type of sales people you recruit and manage will depend on a number of factors. One of these could be whether you sell directly to an end user or whether you manage an indirect channel sales operation. An indirect channel buys your product/service and then sells it on to an end user.

We will now look at:

- What issues are involved in selling through indirect channels
- How your sales people should manage them.

The relationship between the company who makes or supplies the product and the channels/dealers who sell it is important. Your sales people will need a high degree of selling and account management skills.

Challenges and benefits

Many companies trade in this way in order to maximise their market penetration quickly and make use of a channel's relationship with an end user.

Selling in this way can be harder than selling direct because you do not have the same control over the sale. You will therefore need to work with your sales team to develop ways of monitoring a channel's selling activity. This can help them to influence an end user's buying criteria.

Some of the reasons why a channel would want to work with you might include taking advantage of your:

- Brand name
- Product
- Service
- Sales and marketing support.

This is why the channel should sell your products in a way that you like.

Challenges of indirect selling

There are a number of difficult challenges involved in selling through a third party.

These include:

1. Not having a direct dialogue with the end-user (or having total control over the sale)
2. Monitoring whether the channel is promoting your products in a way that you like
3. Getting your own sales people to 'take some responsibility' for the sale
4. The time it can take to introduce new products into their current range
5. Relying on a channel to predict when (and if) sales will actually materialise
6. How likely it is that the channel will remain financially solvent
7. Deciding whether they will be a good partner for you in the future and whether you fit in with their long-term business planning.

These challenges are more easily solved if your sales people are given the skills to develop channel accounts properly.

Therefore, you should ensure that you provide your sales people with:

1. Selling, account management and communication skills
2. An understanding of the indirect channel process
3. Clear guidelines on how to manage an indirect channel.

This will enable each sales person to develop effective relationships at all levels in an indirect channel. It will also help a sales person to influence a channel to sell the number of your products they have planned to.

Meeting the challenge

Your team will need to discuss with you the type of relationship they would like with a channel. This will give them the information needed to plan a sales strategy. You will also be better prepared to review the role of your sales people (dealer/channel managers).

There are a number of aspects you can then review with your channels in order to maximise your selling opportunities. This will include ensuring that they:

1. Sell your product/service correctly
2. Have a high level of on-going training and support
3. Offer sales incentives and promotions
4. Have a regular feedback meeting at all managerial levels in your company
5. Agree an annual forecast volume of business
6. Compare and monitor actual performance against forecast (in order to maintain an agreed pricing structure dealer status).

There has to be a high degree of co-operation and planning in order for both parties to benefit.

Identifying a potential partner

Another important element in maintaining the correct relationship with an indirect channel is to ensure that they match your business objectives. This can include looking at:

- The geographical area they want to cover
- The size and quality of the channel's sales force
- Their sales support functions (tele-sales, marketing, e-commerce)
- Current products in their range
- The ability to hold inventory.

Taking the time to find out this information can help you to assess a dealer's potential to sell your products effectively.

Selling through indirect channels

chapter 11

Benefits of third party relationships

Whatever the challenges involved in selling through a third party, the results can be rewarding and profitable. Your sales team should take advantage of:

1. Greater coverage for your products/service
2. Not having to take direct responsibility for the sale
3. A channel's knowledge and business relationships with an end-user
4. Reduced lead times (by having inventory held by a dealer).

These factors should help your sales people focus on the positive aspects of the business relationship. It can also be a useful reminder to them of what they can expect from a channel in return for using your products/services.

Developing a successful relationship with a dealer requires patience, understanding, good communication and support. If your sales team manage this properly, they can motivate your dealers to meet your objectives.

Managing indirect channels

With this type of sale members of your team will often be referred to as channel/dealer or account managers. Therefore, clearly defined codes of practice are needed to ensure that they support the channel sales operation in the correct way.

Understanding the 3-tier process

Once the buying cycle of the channel and the end user is understood, many of your team's selling skills will need to be applied. It is essential to ensure that they understand the 3-tier (Manufacturer – Channel – End User) process. They also need to have the necessary skills to manage this type of sale.

185

This includes ensuring that they:

- Are properly trained in selling to a third party
- Understand the channel/dealer buying cycle
- Involve your senior management by arranging for them to meet regularly with the largest channel/dealers
- Understand what your competitors do well
- Know if the dealer sells your competitors' products (and the volume).

It is not easy to control the sales behaviour of a channel. They may resent your sales people's interference and may want to retain their independence from you. They are not part of your company and have their own:

- Business plan
- Goals
- Solutions to end user requirements
- Sales targets
- Preferred suppliers.

However, you can maximise your sales opportunities with your indirect channel base by looking at the quality of involvement your sales team achieve with each.

Direct sales

If given a choice, some end users will prefer to deal with a manufacturer directly and not go through an indirect channel. This may be due to previous experience or brand awareness of the product.

It could be down to the end user's perception that they will get a better price or service if they go direct. Whatever the reason, it is up to the channel to establish where the objection has arisen and why. A dealer may require your sales people's help in overcoming any end user objections in this area.

Taking some responsibility for the sale

Individual members of your sales team must take some responsibility for sales to a third party. They need to establish what areas (and accounts) they are able to add value in.

The channel's sales people will need to understand how to sell your product properly in order to fulfil the end user's requirements. The end user must then see the benefit and want to accept the channel's solution.

If this is not done, it can result in the end user not fully appreciating the benefits of your product/service. It can also encourage them to expect a low price (as the channel may not have sold the solution effectively).

Your sales team will need to offer sales initiatives and product support to the channel. This might also involve training/coaching the skills needed to develop their own sales people. This can be particularly useful when a channel is working with larger end user accounts.

Closing a third party sale

Helping a channel close a sale where your products form part of the solution can be difficult. Where your sales people are able to assist in this way, they should ensure that:

- The channel solution matches the end user requirement
- A confirmed timescale has been agreed to close the sale
- The end user has confirmed a budget and will spend the money
- The channel's pricing proposal has been accepted.

This set of criteria is similar to that covered in Chapter 2 – Sales Planning – Forecasting future sales. This is because there is a strong relationship between forecasting a sale and closing one.

An indirect channel may not need your sales people's assistance in these areas. If you are in doubt about their ability to sell your products effectively, what measures can your sales people take? The answer might include:

- Trying to find out in which areas they need help
- Discussing this with the management of both companies (in larger transactions)
- Offering to make end user visits (with the channel)
- Offering more training for the their sales people
- Re-looking at the criteria you expect them to meet.

If channels are managing their business effectively, they may require less sales support. Where their ability to promote your products/service effectively is in doubt, you may need a procedure in place (like a forecasting/account management model).

This will help them monitor how an end user account is being managed. Only then can your sales team determine what is really happening at the end user level and offer the correct type and level of support.

With large end user applications, your sales people can make a significant difference. Companies that form close business relationships with their channels will find it easier to gain acceptance. The more your sales people use their selling skills effectively, the more influence they are likely to have. This is a key element to having a successful indirect channel relationship.

To make any indirect channel relationship work you will need to create a 'win – win – win' situation for all three parties – your company, the channel and the end user.

A review of the relationship should be ongoing. An indirect channel operation will constantly change its focus and expectations (as will your company). You will want to create a partnership approach, which reinforces good practice and improves the way you work together.

Selling through indirect channels

chapter 11

Chapter summary

In this chapter we have looked at 'Selling through indirect channels'. This included:

- Challenges and benefits
- Managing indirect channels.

Selling in this way can be very financially rewarding but it comes with a different set of challenges compared to selling directly to an end user. These need to be properly understood and managed for the partnership to work effectively.

Checklist

✓ Ensure that your strategic aims are in line with those of your channel's.

✓ Encourage your sales people to share responsibility for the sale.

✓ Ensure that you are able to support your channels effectively.

Hawksmere publishing

Hawksmere publishes a wide range of books, reports, special briefings, psychometric tests and videos. Listed below is a selection of key titles.

Other Desktop Guides

The marketing strategy desktop guide
Norton Paley £15.99

Written in a clear, practical style this desktop guide gives a comprehensive understanding of the essential key tools and techniques behind any marketing strategy. It covers the management of your: markets, competitive position, customer behaviour, pricing strategies, products/services, distribution, finance and marketing opportunities.

The credit controller's desktop guide
Roger Mason £15.99

A comprehensive guide to collecting debts effectively, this book covers all aspects of the credit controller's work. Fully up-to-date and written in a clear, practical style, the author, who has considerable experience of credit control for over 20 years, includes case studies, standard letters and forms and an update on the latest legal developments. Key issues covered include: credit control policies, legal action (principles to follow and how to achieve a satisfactory outcome through the courts), as well as factoring, credit agencies and credit insurance.

The company director's desktop guide
David Martin £15.99

This book is essential reading for all directors and professional advisers and will ensure that the reader meets their legal responsibilities, anticipates and resolves problems and works effectively with all parts of the business. The principal areas which are addressed are directors' responsibilities, formal procedures and documents, leadership and management, corporate governance, working with shareholders and public aspects of directorship. Corporate governance in the 21st century is also addressed in this detailed guide.

The company secretary's desktop guide
Roger Mason £15.99

This is a clear comprehensive guide to the complex procedures and legislation governing effective company legislation. All aspects of the Company Secretary's work is covered including share capital, share registration and dividends; accounts and auditors; mergers and acquisitions; profit sharing and share option schemes in addition to voluntary arrangements, administration orders and receivership. This fully up-to-date, practical guide is essential reading for Company Secretaries, Directors, Administrators, Solicitors and Accountants.

The finance and accountancy desktop guide
Ralph Tiffin £15.99

This book, sub-titled, A Handbook for the Non-Financial Manager, is a guide to all aspects of accounting, financial and business literacy. Each chapter is divided into two sections: section one gives a clear insight into the main areas of business and financial accounting, demystifying terms and techniques. The second section should be consulted when a deeper knowledge of that particular topic is required. Also included are examples of standard layouts, as well as review questions with feedback. Invaluable coverage is given on fundamental accounting concepts, cash flow and interpreting financial statements and using ratios, as well as costing and budgeting.

Masters in Management

Mastering business planning and strategy
Paul Elkin £19.99

Mastering financial management
Stephen Brookson £19.99

Mastering leadership
Michael Williams £19.99

Mastering marketing
Ian Ruskin-Brown £22.00

Mastering negotiations
Eric Evans £19.99

Mastering people management
Mark Thomas £19.99

Mastering personal and interpersonal skills
Peter Haddon £19.99

Mastering project management
Cathy Lake £19.99

Essential Guides

The essential guide to buying
and selling unquoted businesses
Ian Smith £29.99

The essential guide to business
planning and raising finance
Naomi Langford-Wood & Brian Salter £29.99

The essential business guide to the Internet
Naomi Langford-Wood & Brian Salter £29.99

Business Action Pocketbooks

Edited by David Irwin

Building your business pocketbook £10.99

Developing yourself and your
staff pocketbook £10.99

Finance and profitability pocketbook £10.99

Managing and employing
people pocketbook £10.99

Sales and marketing pocketbook £10.99

Managing projects and operations
pocketbook £9.99

Effective business communications
pocketbook £9.99

PR techniques that work pocketbook
Edited by Jim Dunn £9.99

Adair on leadership pocketbook
Edited by Neil Thomas £9.99

Other titles

The John Adair handbook
of management and leadership
Edited by Neil Thomas £29.95

The handbook of management fads
Steve Morris £8.95

The inside track to successful management
Dr Gerald Kushel £16.95

The pension trustee's handbook (2nd edition)
Robin Ellison £25

The management tool kit
Sultan Kermally £10.99

Working smarter
Graham Roberts-Phelps £15.99

Test your management skills
Michael Williams £12.95

Boost your company's profits
Barrie Pearson £12.99

The art of headless chicken management
Elly Brewer and Mark Edwards £6.99

Telephone tactics
Graham Roberts-Phelps £9.99

Exploiting IT in business
David Irwin £12.99

EMU challenge and change –
the implications for business
John Atkin £11.99

Everything you need for an
NVQ in management
Julie Lewthwaite £19.99

Sales management and organisation
Peter Green £9.99

Time management and personal development
John Adair and Melanie Allen £9.99

Business health check
Carol O'Connor £12.99

Negotiate to succeed
Edited by Julie Lewthwaite £12.99

Hawksmere also has an extensive range of reports and special briefings which are written specifically for professionals wanting expert information.

For a full listing of all Hawksmere publications, or to order any title, please call Hawksmere Customer Services on 020 7824 8257 or fax on 020 7730 4293.